The Path of Christ

The Path of Christ

Awakening Compassion Within

Suba

© Tobias Moore 2013

www.sohmpublishing.com

SOHM Publishing

The Path of Christ Series: Book 1 of 3

All Rights Reserved. You may copy, print, store, and use this writing as you see fit. My only condition is that I am the only one that makes money on the writing. I wrote the book – so I get the money – that's fair I believe. This and all my writings are free for those who cannot afford them at www.sohmpublishing.com. May you be Blessed☺

Oil Painting on Front Cover: Judy Moore @ www.innerwovenarts.com

ISBN-13: 978-0-9851672-1-9

DEDICATION

To my loving wife. Your support, suggestions, and encouragement gave me the means to unfold myself. Thank you…

CONTENT

Introduction — 9

Chapter 1   Preparing the Field   13
- Preciousness of Life
- Impermanence
- Reaping what we Sow
- Narrowness of the Path

Chapter 2   Planting the Seeds of Christ   33
- Poor
- Mourning
- Meek
- Hunger and Thirst
- Merciful
- Pure of Heart
- Peacemakers
- Persecuted

Chapter 3   Rooting the Mind   53
- Being Focused
- Being Content
- Being free of Jealousy
- Being free of Judgment
- Being free of Expectations
- Being Joyful
- Being Sacred

Chapter 4   Growing from Practice   75
- Knowledge
- Virtue
- Giving/Charity
- Patience
- Perseverance
- Temperance
- Humbleness
- Kindness
- Tranquility
- Wisdom

Chapter 5   Cultivating the Path   107
- Adversity into a Practice
- Becoming like a Child
- Faith

Chapter 6   Flowing through Meditation   119
- Contemplation
- Concentration

Chapter 7   Awakening Compassion   129
                   Creating Open Space
                   Connecting with the Feeling
                   Personalizing
                   Universalizing

Appendix I   Year Study Plan   137

Appendix II   Secondary Practices   153
                   Anger
                   Love
                   Forgiveness
                   Prayer

Appendix III   Essential Teachings of Jesus 179

Bibliography

Thank you Yeshua for showing us the way!

Introduction

This text is dedicated to those who desire to embody the teachings of Jesus. If you have come to this book with the belief that it will make you feel good about yourself or justify your religious beliefs – return it. This text is not for entertainment, nor will it make you feel good about yourself; this work is a practical manual for those who seek to awaken the Christos within: to do that – we must let go of our limited self-concepts.

The four practices in chapter one help clear away many of our misconceptions regarding happiness, in addition, they help free us from core beliefs that prevent us from walking the Path of Christ. The most important thing necessary to start walking the Path is to appreciate life. To honor and give thanks for the blessings and beauty surrounding us at all times. Once we have an appreciation of life, we can begin to recognize the impermanence of life and how our stable, solid perception of reality we hold onto creates suffering in our lives. As we begin to understand the temporariness of life our desires and attachments start to soften. The third practice in chapter one deals with reaping what we have sown. This seed practice guides us towards righteousness and away from unwholesomeness. When we have gained an understanding of these three practices we naturally come to realize how narrow the Path – that the Path to fulfillment is incredibly difficult.

The second chapter plants the Seeds of Christ within our hearts and minds. These seeds are the core teachings Jesus taught on the Mount: poor, mourning, meek, hungering and thirsting for righteousness, mercy, purity, peacefulness, and persecution. These pithy teachings give rise to humbleness, thankfulness, simplicity, spiritual yearning, mercy, purity, peace, and resolve.

Chapter three introduces the practices that help these Seeds grow in our lives by rooting them deep within us. Each of the seven practices in this chapter deal with an aspect of our mind's ability to liberate or imprison itself. The first and most valuable practice in chapter three is learning to focus – to control our thoughts and focus our attention solely on that which is before us. The second practice helps us find contentment with who we are and with what state we are in. The next three practices address three of the greatest causes of suffering in our lives: jealousy, judgment, and expectations. When we learn to let go of these three things we find peace, freedom, and openness. Following these practices we find it easier to invite a joyful mind. And in living joyfully, we find ourselves living in a sacred manner.

Having gained an understanding of the Path, acquired the necessary tools to walk the Path, and started to cultivate right thinking, chapter four leads us to a true understanding of the Christ Path. In this chapter there are ten key practices to work with. Each practice builds off of the others so as to lead us to the culmination of the Path. First we acquire a true understanding of Jesus' instructions, then we cultivate virtuous action. Through virtue we learn to give and share. Through sharing we gain patience, and with patience, comes the need for perseverance. The more we work with these areas the more temperate and balanced we become in all areas of our lives: physically, emotionally, mentally, socially, energetically, and spiritually. This balance gives rise to true humility; a state of being that is soft and open. Through humility comes tranquility and through tranquility comes wisdom.

To help us grow on the Path and to nurture the seeds we have planted we use the three cultivators in chapter five. The first practice is learning to turn every moment, trial, adversity, struggle, pain, loss, difficulty, and any other unwanted situation into a practice. The second is learning to become a child once again - not in ignorance, but in innocence, openness, curiosity, and freshness. The last practice in this chapter is faith. While this might seem to be the easiest of the three, in truth, it is one of the hardest practices – to have faith as small as a mustard seed: to move mountains – do you know anyone that can move mountains?

Chapter six introduces the basic principles of concentration and contemplation meditation in order to set the foundation for the compassion practice in chapter seven. The text ends with three appendixes: a one year study plan for working with this text; four secondary practices (anger, love, forgiveness, prayer) that help deepen our experience on the Path; and lastly, the essential teachings of Jesus that ought to be memorize and embody as we walk our Path.

How to use this book

There are three things you can do to reap the benefits of this book. The first is to read and think over what is said. Avoid mindless reading. Take your time and contemplate upon each part. Answer every question and do every project. Write down your research, opinions, ideas, thoughts, and feelings into a journal/notebook. This journal will become a useful tool to help you along on your Path.

The second thing you can do to enliven these words is to memorize the quotes of Jesus used in this text. If you have the time, read the gospels and remember other verses as well. For although i have tried to gather the more pertinent sayings of Jesus, there are hundreds of others that can help you in your life. Once memorized, these root sayings will come to memory whenever you need empowerment, support, and guidance.

The last thing that will help you reap the benefits of this book is to do the practices in each chapter and record in the journal your successes and failures. When a sincere effort is applied toward these and similar practices, the qualities of Christ will naturally blossom within you.

Forewarning

The Problem with this book is not that something new is being said. The problem is that it puts the responsibility of salvation in our own hands. In order to follow the Path Jesus shared with us we will eventually have to let go of our desires, goals, motivations, and turn to face the light of GOD. This is extremely difficult to achieve.

The beautiful thing about this book is that it does not expect anything from the reader. Take as you wish and be blessed.

Blessed are those who hear the words of Jesus and understand.

Chapter One
Preparing the Field

- Preciousness of Life
- Impermanence
- Reaping what we Sow
- Narrowness of the Path

The four contemplations of this chapter help strengthen us on our Christian Path. Without these contemplations there is a tendency for our hearts to resist and our minds to find ways to diminish the teachings of Jesus. These four preliminary contemplations enable us to see how important it is to grow in compassion and not waste our lives in frivolous quests to fulfill endless desires.

When we recognize how precious life is, we naturally strive to utilize every waking moment to awaken the Christos within us. With the awareness of impermanence, we learn to let go of our material desires by cultivating an enlightened mind and a compassionate heart. By understanding the ramifications of our actions, we seek to develop positive actions and eliminate unwholesome ones. As we become aware of the narrowness of the Path, we start to really take the teachings of Jesus more seriously.

The Preciousness of Life

The very hairs of your head are all numbered. (Matthew 10:30)

If this is so, then every breath and every moment in our lives is to be cherished and directed towards awakening the divine within us. We should always be thankful for the good fortunes we have. If we cannot see, we should be thankful for what we can hear. If we have no feet to walk upon, we should be thankful for what we can touch. If we cannot move, we should be thankful for what we can think and dream. How much more thankful should we be when we have all these things given unto us?

If we have a healthy body, have leisure time, are born in a place where there is nurturing and little violence, are taught about Jesus and his teachings, and can see the teachings being practiced, then we have a great opportunity to practice and awaken the Christos within us *(These are the Five Factors of a Blessed Life)*.

> **Seek ye the kingdom of GOD; and all these things shall be added unto you.** *(Luke 12:31)*

This Kingdom of GOD is not some faraway place – it is here and now. It is a state of being and a level of awareness that brings us closer to the Divine. One tool we have at our finger tips to awaken the Kingdom is thankfulness.

Thankfulness opens the doors of abundance by giving us the opportunity to invite a deeper awareness to every facet of our lives. While temporary pleasures come and go, the underlining joy that resides in every moment expands and lengthens in duration. When we are grateful, this underlining joy brings our attention to the blessings we have rather than the things we lack.

In addition, gratitude softens our hearts and builds our capacity for forgiveness. It strengthens our immune system and improves our way of relating with the world – not only physically, but mentally, emotionally, socially, energetically, and spiritually as well.

Of course, just because we are thankful does not get rid of life's hardships or stop us from stubbing our toe, getting stuck in traffic, or watching someone we love die. While it does not protect us from life's underbelly, it does help soften life's ups and downs, it helps us keep our hearts and minds open to receiving, and it shows us the good that can come from the bad.

Things to contemplate:

"The very hairs of your head are all numbered." (Matthew 10:30)
- Just visualize a hair on a piece of grass or a crevasse on a speck of sand and know that no hair or crevasse in the whole world from the beginning of the earth will ever be the same. Go outside and pick up a speck of sand to see for yourself.
- Everyone and everything is precious – even our enemies.
- What does a precious life mean to you? What do you think it means to others?

"Seek ye the kingdom of GOD; and all these things shall be added unto you." (Luke 12:31)
- What is the Kingdom of GOD?
- What will be added?
- How can you seek the Kingdom of GOD?

"In everything give thanks." (I Thessalonians 5:18)
- Should you be thankful for bad things that happen to you? Why or why not?
- What emotions are connected with thankfulness?
- What is the opposite of thankfulness? What emotions are connected with that?
- How can bad things turn into good things? Does thankfulness help or hinder this process?

Practices to help invite thankfulness:

- Make a list of all the things you are thankful for: people, things, experiences, knowledge, et cetera. Then take a moment sometime during the week to open your heart to each of these things. To do this, start by thinking of the object. Bring all your awareness to the object and then mentally note being thankful for it. The more you think about it, the more feeling will arise towards it. It is through this feeling that true gratefulness arises. Take another moment during the week to consider what your life would be like without one of the more important things on your list. Allow those emotions to deepen your gratitude towards it.
- As you sit down every day this week for dinner, mentally and/or verbally note all the things you are thankful for during your day.

- Whenever you feel like life is weighing you down and gratefulness is on the other side of the world – take a breath – and be thankful. During these moments the power of thankfulness really becomes apparent. Start with acknowledging the unpleasant experience or situation and then move the mind towards being grateful. This does not stop horrible things from happening, but it does shift your perspective and opens you to experiencing happiness in situations that before only invited suffering.

Impermanence

> *Lay not up for yourselves treasures upon earth, where moth and rust doth corrupt, and where thieves break through and steal.* (Matthew 6:19)

Impermanence is a state where nothing remains the same: what is built will ultimately fall, what is born will die, and what comes together will eventually separate. We hold desperately to security and stability, but it only takes one thief, a fire, some natural disaster, or someone leaving our life to change everything. We can be on top of the world one day and have the world upon our back the next. Contemplating upon impermanence strengthens our resolve to embrace each moment in our life. To become fully conscious and aware of what is going on around and within us. Life is too short to live as a robot.

In Luke 12:37 Jesus teaches us to be vigilant and diligent in the face of impermanence, for life keeps moving no matter how much we wish otherwise. This is the reason why we contemplate impermanence. When change comes, we can find peace and balance within it.

There are four areas of impermanence to consider: physical, emotional, mental, and social. We can see how impermanence manifests in the physical world through the seasons, ageing, sickness, and death. In the emotional world we can see impermanence through the constant fluctuation of the feelings and emotional experiences. One moment we might be peacefully driving down the highway, and in the next moment, a great rage ignites within us because we are cut off by another driver. Where did the peace go? Mentally it is easy to see how fickle and impermanent our thoughts are by simply trying to hold onto one thought or image in exclusion to all others. Another aspect of mental impermanence is our beliefs, for just like a child whose understandings of the world changes as they grow older, so our understandings of the Divine will change as we become more Christlike. Lastly, from the social perspective, we meet new people, friends move away, family members die, we change jobs, and so on.

Within these four areas are three times of reference: past, present, and future. The past is always behind us, the future is constantly coming, and the present is but a moment in time that never remains – even when we want it to. There are only two unchanging things in life. One is impermanence, for change will always happen, and the other is the eternal present moment.

When we understand the essence of impermanence we find ourselves no longer holding onto our attachments with such vigor. Our faith and efforts strengthen and our lives become enriched with great equanimity as we let go of our concepts and beliefs and open ourselves to the moment without any reservation or limitation.

Things to contemplate:

"Lay not up for yourselves treasures upon earth, where moth and rust doth corrupt, and where thieves break through and steal." (Matthew 6:19)

- Watch the earth change.
- Contemplate the loss of a family member, friend, or possession.
- Try to hold an image in your mind for a few minutes.
- Think about a few times when your emotions fluctuated between extremes.
- Consider how material things decay, get lost, destroyed, or otherwise disappear.
- How does the recognition of impermanence help you let go and be present?

Practices to help you recognize impermanence:

- Write down anything in this world that is permanent. How is that list coming along? Is there anything of yourself that is forever unchanging? If you say your beliefs – then is there nothing left for you to learn about the Divine?
- Make a list of how you see impermanence in your life: physically, emotionally, mentally, socially, desires, beliefs, etc…
- Spend a few nights this week actively investigating how impermanence plays a role in your life. What things were exciting before but are now mundane; what relationships have come and gone; what things did you yearn for before but now neglect or even despise? Be creative as you work with this practice. Really try to understand the principle of impermanence.
- After finishing your investigation spend at least one day this week looking at the world around you. Open your eyes and see through the lens of impermanence. See the cars moving, the wind, the conversations, the thoughts – look at everything with the intention of recognizing how impermanence plays a role in your life.

Reaping what we Sow

What measure you mete it shall be measured unto you again. (Matthew 7.2)

If the above verse is true, then we should always seek positive actions and dissolve negative ones. While many of us might concede the possibility that this saying is true, the problem with it is the elusive nature in which it manifests. Too many of us have witnessed bad people living good lives while good people get screwed. How can we account for this discrepancy?

The easiest answer is heaven and hell. They might not get punished this life, but the next will be their ruin. This belief sounds great, but there is something about it that does not resonate with modern sentiment; especially when a bad person can be on their death bed, ask for forgiveness and open their heart to Jesus – and all is well. Screw that!

Thankfully, there is another possibility, and we can prove its validity in our lives directly. We do not need faith to see it, all we have to do is open our eyes and observe the world around us. When we are mean to friends, what is the consequence? Often times they are mean back or even stop being our friends.

One misunderstanding that arises with this immutable law is that it does not always come back to us the exact way we dished it out. In fact, because of the uniqueness of life, it never comes back in the exact same way. One way to look at it is to see a scale that we have placed dirt clods on – we can put dirt clods on the other side of the scale until it balances out or we can take a giant crap on top till the scales even out. The point is, when we send out negativity, we will get it back – and it aint always coming back the way we expect it to – especially when we are okay with our actions and do not fear the ramifications of them.

Being mean to others does not necessarily imply others will be mean to us. It could happen, but it might not as well. What it does mean is that sending out negativity will bring in negativity. Our friends might not be mean to us, but they might stop being our friends. They might sabotage us, talk about us behind our back, create tension with our other relationships – the possibilities are endless. The point is that every action has a consequence in the real world (actio et reactio): it might not always be apparent, but when we look, we can see it.

In order to properly contemplate this rule we need to know the three channels it manifests through: action, speech, and thought.

Actions

Four basic physical aspects of this law are highlighted in the tenets of the Ten Commandments: Thou shall not kill, steal, covet, and adultery. Jesus tells us that when we do something to others we do it to ourselves (Matthew 7:12). He speaks on the effects of physical aggression and violence in the following verses:

Harming

> *All they that take the sword shall perish with the sword.* (Matthew 26:55)

While there are many verses that forbid murder and harming others, this one speaks directly to Christians because it forbids harmful actions even at the cost of being persecuted. When we are violent, aggressive, and hurtful, we cause suffering to ourselves and others. Stand in front of a wall and throw a brick as hard as you can – what is the consequence? The brick harms the wall and bounces off to hurt us.

Stealing

> *Let him that stole steal no more: but rather let him labor working with his hands the things which is good, that he may have to give to him that needeth.* (Ephesians 4:28)

Stealing comes in many guises. It can be as simple as stealing a pen or lighter, from using the copy machine at work for selfish reasons, downloading a program, music, or movie from the internet, taking the best of something from another when we have the opportunity to take the lesser portion or value, and of course, stealing can arise simply from the act of taking something from a person or group of people without their permission or knowledge. The act of stealing comes from a state of inadequacy or obsession, and from a desire for power, control, money, excitement, and/or things.

Coveting

> *Ye cannot serve GOD and Mammon.* (Luke 16:8-13)

Mammon is the god of luxury, possessions, riches, and all those physical desires we constantly seek to acquire and possess. Jesus is adamant about the things of this world and how they bring loss and worry; instead of yearning after these things he tells us to strive for heavenly treasures:

> *Lay up for yourselves treasures in heaven. For where your treasure is, there will your heart be also.* (Matthew 6:20-21)

We cannot take this world with us when we die. So let us not be like the rich man who horded all his grain for the day when he could retire (Luke 12:16-20). This does not mean we have to give up all our desires and simply live as an ascetic in a cave. What it means is that we walk the Path as far as we can. The Christ Path is hard, so we should avoid self-degradation when we fall short of it; as the old saying goes: "It is not how many times we fall that defines us; it is how many times we pick ourselves back up." The idea that we can wake up one day and our desires, attachments, and greed are gone is very attractive – but not realistic. The key is to take heed of our covetous nature and be vigilant against it.

> *Take heed, and beware of covetousness: for a man's life consisteth not in the abundance of the things which he possesses.* (Luke 12:15)

This verse attacks the core value of western culture; a big house, white picket fence, and all the amenities of life say nothing of the inner nature of our being. We can own everything in the world and still be unhappy and miserable. Some of these things are nice to have, but to allow them to control our lives or to define us, takes us away from the Path Jesus shared with us.

Sexual misconduct

> *That whosoever looketh on a woman to lust by them hath committed adultery with her already in his heart.* (Matthew 5:28)

This is a hard one for some of us. I have problems with it myself. Thank goodness there are many ways to work with and transform lustful energy. The first step is to become consciously aware of having the thoughts; not just experiencing them, but actually bringing the awareness to the fact that we are having them while in the mist of them – not afterwards. The second thing is to utilize one or more of the following techniques:

- Consider the outcome of such thoughts and what they really do for you. Does fantasying manifest the actual act or is there something else to it?
- Remember past experiences of getting what you sought and how quickly you moved to the next thing once the thrill diminished.
- Think about how she or he would feel if they could see and hear what is going on in your mind.
- Dwell upon the fact that GOD sees what you are thinking and doing right at that moment.
- Think upon this person as a sister, brother, child, mother, or father.
- Contemplate what is under the skin rather than its external form: blood, pus, sinew, phlegm, excrement, etc...
- Think about what Jesus would do under the same circumstance.
- Focus on different aspects of the person in order to shift your mind away from the lustful energy.
- Set a resolve or goal in which you seek to embody the qualities of Christ within yourself and then bring that resolve to mind whenever the feeling of desire awakens within you.
- Know that your body is the Temples of the Spirit and to waste your energy hampers the Spirit from awaking within you *(1 Corinthians 6:15)*.
- Every time you take a bath or shower, visualize and verbalize the water washing away the desire and see it actually happen.
- When the lustful desire arises think of something that makes you angry or frustrated. Once the lustful desire dissolves, turn your attention to the anger. While this technique seems to be counterproductive, in practice it is easier to deal with anger than lust. The beautiful thing about anger is that it burns away any other emotion.

- When you are caught in the moment of desire either pray for strength or repeat the name of Jesus over and over again until the energy of desire disperses.
- Set a resolve to banish all desireful thoughts from the mind, and then when they arise, literally push them out with your will – the more you work with this, the easier it gets.
- Transmute the energy by bringing the full attention to the heart and breathing into it until the energy rises from the loins – shifting the energy and the thoughts.

Speech

> *Every idle word that men shall speak, they shall give account thereof in the day of judgment.* (Matthew 12:36)

If we are held accountable for every idle word that comes from our mouth, how much more accountable will we be when we slander, lie, deceive, gossip, chatter, bare false witness, and speak offensively to others? We should always be mindful of what we say and we should always contemplate on the effect our words have on others. When we slander someone by speaking evil of them or subtly saying things that turn others against them: what good does that do? Does it *really* make us happier, stronger, or better?

> *Not that which goeth into the mouth defileth a man; but that which cometh out of the mouth, this defileth a man.* (Matthew 15:11)

When we gossip about others: what good does that do? Who can trust us when we speak so freely about others behind their back? Might those who share in the gossip also talk about us or listen to others talk about us when we are not around?

It is better to hold the tongue than to lie. Lying is a never ending spiral that eventually causes us to lose one of the greatest things of life: trust. Lying is a hopeless addiction that only gets stronger the more we do it. The best way to overcome it is to avoid it.

What are we doing when we use offensive speech, talk cruelly to others, and say sarcastic and biting words to cause suffering? How do we feel when such is done to us?

Thoughts

> *These people draweth nigh unto me with their mouth, and honoureth me with their lips; but their heart is far from me. (Matthew 15:8)*

Our thoughts are the lens we see the world through. When we feel bad, we tend to have negative thoughts; when we have bad thoughts, we tend to feel bad. Also, when we have bad thoughts, bad things seem to arise more often in our lives: we stub our toe, people avoid us, and the light always seems to be red.

Thoughts also limit the world around us. When we think a person is a liar, then every word that comes from their mouth is a lie. If we have been led to believe someone is a bad person, then even if they do nice things, we tend to think badly of them.

Another facet of thought is its ability to hold and feed emotions. For example, someone cuts us off on the highway: surprise, fear, anxiety, and excitement arise. Then the thoughts come. If we feel relief, this usually ends the situation. Anger on the other hand, being fed by the flames of blame exasperate the situation. If these thoughts continue, it can really ruin our day.

So from physical actions to our thoughts, we are held accountable for everything we do, say, and think. If "every hair on our head is counted," so much more is every thought, word, and deed remembered. The Christ Path is not an easy Path to walk and anyone who tells us differently is trying to make us buy or join something. The Christ Path is one of the noblest things we can do as a human here on earth.

And so, we first need to work on our actions by stopping those things that cause unbalance and disharmony within our lives. As we gain control over our actions we can start to gain control over our words and how we use them: speaking only with truth, honesty, and harmony. As we harness our speech, so our minds begin to settle down, becoming more focused and aware. The more alert our minds become, the more energy arises within our life. This energy is what gives us the strength, stamina, and support to continue walking the Path.

Things to contemplate:

"What measure you mete it shall be measured unto you again." (Matthew 7.2)
- Do you believe this? Why or why not?
- Is there anything wrong with being a miser?
- What about the boss who is a tyrant: does he/she get what she/he wants?

"An eye for an eye, and a tooth for a tooth: but I say unto you, that ye resist not evil: but whatsoever shall smite thee on thy right cheek, turn him the other also." (Matthew 5:38-39)
- Think about hitting another person – will they not hit you back or maybe get you sent to jail?
- Why would Jesus say turn the other cheek? What does that mean?
- What is the ultimate lesson here? To hold onto physical things, acquire possessions, and grasp for any desire that pops its head into your consciousness? Or is there something else?

"Ye cannot serve GOD and Mammon." (Luke 16:8-13)
- Does Jesus support the effort to acquire possessions, wealth, reputation, etc? When you answer this do not look at Paul's writings to justify your answer, look only to what Jesus said and see what you find.
- Is the physical world different from the spiritual world? Explain answer.
- Does fame and wealth reflect a person's spiritual attainments? If so, who? Out of all the millionaires alive, how many?
- Name one really important figure in religious history. How much money did they possess? With this question in mind, find someone that lived at least a few hundred years back. One reason for this is that it would be easy to look at those who live now and see how rich they are, only to find out a hundred years from now that their name is all but forgotten or who they really were did not come out

26 Preparing the Field

until their death. By looking to those who lived hundreds of years ago you can bypass both of these problems.

"Lay up for yourselves treasures in heaven. For where your treasure is, there will your heart be also." (Matthew 6.20-21)
- What are the treasures of heaven? Are they physical possessions, the number of people you converted, or something else?
- What rules your life? Your boss, teachers, partners, companions, friends, parents, children, or maybe your goals, intentions, thoughts, and desires?
- Is it the possessions that define a person or what a person does with what they have?

"Take heed, and beware of covetousness: for a man's life consisteth not in the abundance of the things which he possesses." (Luke 12:15)
- Why is this different from what society and many churches portray?
- Are possessions good, bad, or maybe a little of both? Explain answer?
- What is your stance on possessions? What is the stance Jesus takes on possessions? What about Paul? What is the difference between all these different stances? What is the same?
- What do you covet? Money, T.V., keeps sake, opinions, beliefs, ideas, etc?

"Let him that stole steal no more: but rather let him labor working with his hands the things which is good, that he may have to give to him that needeth." (Ephesians 4:28)
- What are some justifications for stealing?
- Is recording a movie stealing? What about using the copy machine at work or sampling food at the grocery store?
- Have you stolen anything? Why did you do it?
- Have you been stolen from? How did you feel?
- How does stealing prevent you from being content?

"That whosoever looketh on a woman to lust by them hath committed adultery with her already in his heart" (Matthew 5:28)
- While this verse talks about lustfulness, how could it apply to greed or any other type of desire that pulls your thoughts? If by thinking lustfully after another you have already commit adultery, could this also apply to everything you think about? Lust is not only a word for sexual desire, but any strong desire that seeks to consume and control you.

- Make a list of your top twenty desires.
- What happens when you desire something?
- How do you feel about masturbating? What feelings arise after doing it? Relief, dirty, relaxed, agitated, empowered, embarrassed, sinful, nothing, etc?

"Every idle word that men shall speak, they shall give account thereof in the day of judgment" (Matthew 12:36)
- What is the day of judgment?
- Every word! Think about that.
- Slander, gossip, lying, distorting, misdirecting, glazing over, yelling, deception, hurtful words?
- Why do you speak? When you speak is it to enlighten, entertain, convey information, control others, uplift, downgrade? What do you want and expect in your interactions with others?
- Sometimes it is not what you say but how you say things? What does this mean to you?
- Why do people slander and gossip? Do you? Why or why not?

"Not that which goeth into the mouth defileth a man; but that which cometh out of the mouth, this defileth a man." (Matthew 15:11)
- This verse is talking about unclean hands and food, but it also goes much further than that. What does it say to you?
- Of course you can watch a bunch of violent movies and eat junk food all day and only have pure thoughts and a healthy body – it is possible – but unlikely.
- What does this verse teach you regarding judgment?

"These people draweth nigh unto me with their mouth, and honoureth me with their lips; but their heart is far from me." (Matthew 15:8)
- What does the heart represent?
- What is Jesus talking about when he says, "they draweth nigh with their mouth and honoureth me with their lips?" Who does this apply to?
- What do you think about mostly? The Divine or your life? Is it what you need, want, have to do, or some other thing like that, or is it the welfare of others? How often do you think about spiritual things? All the time, half the time, at church, or never?
- Suppose that a person does everything according to the scripture – they say and act in perfect accord with the Bible: might this verse still apply to them? Explain.
- What relationship does this verse have with works?

Practices to help sow good seeds:

- Write down one big decision you made recently. After you do that, trace the source of your decision. Why did you make it? What things did you consider? Who was involved? Next, write down the outcome. How did that decision affect/effect others? What were some of the wanted and unwanted ramifications? How does making this decision effect similar decisions you will make in the future? When you can answer these and similar questions before you make choices in your life, you will find yourself making wiser choices.
- For one day write down every decision you make. From the cloths you wear to the food you eat, to warming and parking the car to when you go to sleep. Why did you say this or that? The reason for this exercise is to help you break the robotic behavior patterns that rule your life. Not only does this practice help you see the patterns in your life, it will help you see new ways of being.
- Every time you become aware of a negative or hurtful thought, look at it and then chase it away. To do this, sometimes all that is needed is to want the thought to go away, other times you might have to forcefully remove it by shifting the way you look at the situation or even shifting your awareness to another object altogether. Some thoughts just keep coming back, and sometimes you will not be able to get rid of them. They will just eat away at you, and that is okay. The mind takes a lifetime to control, so relax and do not belittle yourself. Just keep trying. The more you work on this, the less power the monkey mind will have.

The Narrowness of the Path

> **Strait is the gate, and narrow is the way, which leadeth unto life, and few there be that find it.**
> *(Matthew 7:14)*

Finding the way is difficult – staying on it is even harder. Just to put this Narrow Path into perspective the following list gives us a sense of how many obstacles there are on the path: lust, anger, conceit, mistaken beliefs, doubt, excessive attachments, jealousy, greed, ill will, sloth, restlessness, hatred, judgment, hubris, fear, lying, and on and on the list can go.

So what is this verse saying? Why is it hard to find a way that leads unto life? Part of the answer is that there is no systematic approach to the teachings of Jesus. What is the goal of Christianity? To go to heaven? How do we get there? By believing in Jesus as the only son of God who died for our sins, going to church once a week, giving to charity, being baptized, and trying not to screw up too much – and if we do – then asking for forgiveness is all it takes to make things right with GOD. This sounds like a parent's dream come true: if their children recognized the suffering the parents go through on their behalf, if they (children) have faith that what their parents say is in their best interest, that they listen and follow the rules, share, and when they screw up, say sorry and deal with the consequences – what more can a parent ask for? Well, there is actually a lot more a parent can desire, such as their children being healthy, happy, intelligent, creative, et cetera. But that is not the point. In general parents are content when their children get along and are happy.

This sounds easy, but then, why does Jesus say there are few "that find it?" The key is to have a goal, an ideal, a person to look up to and emulate. Believing in Jesus gives us that person. We know he did it. We know he told us we could do it. And we know from his words the things we need to do. And yet, here most of us sit caught-up in life's many distractions. We can know the whole Bible by heart, believe in Jesus and what he taught us, and if we are still shackled down by these obstructions, we will be the many – not the few. Knowledge and desire is not enough. Action is the missing link. Without action it is all for nothing. As Jesus says: these "people draweth nigh unto me with their mouth, and honoureth me with their lips; but their heart is far from me" (Matthew 15:8).

For those who wish to be more than a weekend Christians, the first step is to want it. For those who are happy with the way things are, that is okay – even Jesus was okay with it. He told the rich man all he had to do was follow the Ten Commandments and he would have eternal life (Matthew 19:16-19). In other words, just be a good person and life after life will be yours. "Give to him that asketh thee" (Matthew 5:42), be humble and take the lower seat (Luke 14:8-11), follow the Commandments, and all will be well. On the other hand, if we want to find the Strait Gate and walk the Narrow Path, then we have to do more than that. We have to become perfect as Jesus instructed us to do. It is not easy – but it is possible – for why would Jesus claim it to be otherwise? We can always interpret his words pessimistically, but that would mean it is all subjective: Jesus either meant what he said or he did not. It is that simple.

Things to contemplate:

"Strait is the gate, and narrow is the way, which leadeth unto life, and few there be that find it." (Matthew 7:14)
- How is it that Christianity has the largest number of members and still there will be few that find the way?
- What does "find it" mean?
- What is "life" pertaining to?

"Give to him that asketh thee." (Matthew 5:42)
- Christianity is a religion of giving: GOD gives, Jesus gives, the saints give, and every human is told to give to each other.
- When do you give?
- Name a few opportunities of giving you failed to take.

"He that is greatest among you shall be your servant." (Matthew 23:11)
- Is this what you are taught in society? If so, give some examples.
- Is this what you are taught in church? If so, give some examples.
- What does it mean to be taught anyways? Just listening to someone give a sermon? Maybe learn techniques and practices to apply? Give some examples.
- What does it mean, "The greatest among you shall be your servant?" How are you taught this in your life? Who shows it to you? Nobody? Everybody?
- Would Jesus be taken advantage of today?
- What exactly is this verse talking about?

Practices to help realize the Narrowness of the Path:

- Make a list of all the things in this book you fall short on – this is vital to your growth: "Physician, heal thyself" sums it up (Luke 4:23).
- Do you know anyone on the strait path? Give reasons why you think they are so.
- List two times you had good intentions to do something and yet found yourself unable to manifest your intentions, or even did the opposite of what you intended. Explain how this can interrelate with the Straight and Narrow Path? What did these two situations teach you?

Conclusion

Notice how each preliminary thought motivates us to become more aware of life. By recognizing the preciousness of life we come to realize our great blessings, which in turn, helps us avoid wasting those precious moments we have to help ourselves and others. Contemplating on impermanence helps us to embrace life and at the same time not be so attached to it. Reaping what we sow shows us that our actions have consequences and that by striving towards the good we will stop going down roads that lead to negative repercussions. Instead we will be doing those things that help calm our minds and create a good atmosphere from which we can continue to grow and become more compassionate. And by understanding the Narrowness of the Path, we are pushed to be vigilant and aware of those things that cause harm or even divert us from the Path. Each of these preliminary exercises help keep our minds focused and our efforts directed towards that which furthers our growth.

There are three things we can do to help sink these four practices into our consciousness. The first action we can take is to acquire a full understanding of what these terms mean. What does it mean to reap what we sow? What is impermanence, a precious life, a narrow path? After we grasp these terms with a deeper understanding we can then begin to investigate our lives to see if these concepts contradict what we see and experience. For example, can we see that our actions cause a reaction and come back to affect/effect us? Can we see how life slowly ages and dies out, or that at one time this person or business was on top of the world one moment and now are gone? How about some of the blessings that we have in our lives: how many of us have shelter and food to feed our families? What about the street person who has all the time in the world to burn? For some of us this might be hard to see, we might be dying of some terminal illness or starving in some desolate place. The idea of this practice is to realize that at this moment we have a second to breathe in life and be thankful enough to try opening ourselves up to relate with the world directly.

After we see the effects these four teachings have in our lives we can begin to meditate on them. We can look at life through them in order to help us further awaken to the Christian Path. The idea behind these four meditations is to give us strength to exchange our old habits and behaviors (wineskins) for those which bring happiness, peace, wisdom, compassion, and knowledge into our lives. They help us utilize everything we have in our power to walk with Jesus and to carry our own cross. For just like John who carried the cross for Jesus, we can help Jesus with the burden of the cross by carrying our own.

Chapter Two
Planting the Seeds of Christ

- Poor
- Mourning
- Meek
- Hunger and Thirst after Righteousness
- Merciful
- Pure of Heart
- Peacemakers
- Persecuted

The following eight practices come from the Sermon on the Mount. These eight teachings contain the core essence of the Christian Path. They are the seeds we plant within our hearts and nurture with our prayers and practices. The roots that grow from these practices awaken softness within our lives and aid us in becoming more open, compassionate, and understanding.

When we recognize our poorness in Spirit, we are driven to awaken the teachings of Jesus within our lives. As we mourn for what we have lost, we find comfort in the things we have in our lives. With meekness and humbleness we find abundance and enjoyment in life. By searching for righteousness we are filled to the brim with truth and understanding. As mercy awakens within us, we find rest from all our troubles. With a pure heart we are given new eyes to experience the universe with. By becoming peacemakers, we learn how to follow in the footsteps of Jesus. And when we are persecuted for walking the Christian Path (both internally and externally), we are strengthened and empowered to carry onward.

As we gain a deeper understanding of these practices and learn how to embody them in our lives, we obtain some of the greatest blessings in life: we receive the Kingdom of Heaven, comfort from all our troubles, abundance, truth and wisdom, enjoyment, unity, and freedom. These gifts come naturally when we unfold these practices in our lives.

Poor

> *Blessed are the poor in spirit: for theirs is the kingdom of heaven.* (Matthew 5:3)
>
> *Blessed be ye poor: for yours is the kingdom of God.* (Luke 6:20)

How many times have we heard people speak on the merits of humility and simplicity but never see it in action? Why is that? This first Beatitude spoken on the Mount is the source from which all the other Beatitudes grow from. It touches on both our spiritual and physical egos. One deals with our desire for physical possessions and the other with hubris and the overflowing egotism of being spiritual and knowing everything spiritual. This verse helps us see the propensity of our minds and bodies towards excessiveness, attachment, desire, aversion, and fear.

This Beatitude helps us understand the simple principle of desire: the more we acquire, the more we want. One day it will be a VCR, then a DVD player, a DVD recorder, a combination of them, and so on and so forth. After we acquire these things our desires move on towards wanting something bigger, better, and more expensive. At some point it should stop – but does it? It is an unquestionable thirst that is never filled:

> *Whosoever drinketh of this water shall thirst again. But, whosoever drinketh of the water that I shall give him shall never thirst; but the water that I shall give him shall be in him a well of water springing up into everlasting life.* (John 4:13-14)

Eventually what we find in our search to fulfill our desires is that there is nothing physical that can satisfy our hunger. The only thing that quenches our thirst is a state of being that comes through our spiritual evolution. This evolution does not arise from the intellectual spirituality we see in the world; rather, it comes from the application of the teachings within our daily lives. As we learn how to apply the teachings we begin to see our desires dissolve on their own accord. As the desires loosen their choke hold on us, the more aware we become of the abundance that we have in our lives: for every little thing becomes great – and this greatness is more encompassing and fulfilling than the greatest happiness that comes from acquiring things. This way of thinking is foreign and counter to what we are taught in the world as Jesus tells us in John:

> *If ye were of the world, the world would love his own: but, because ye are not of the world, but I have chosen you out of the world, therefore the world hateth you.* (15:19)

A question that comes to mind when we talk about letting go of desire is: "How can we get to that point in our life?" One thing we can do is be content with what we have. Not to work for our desires, but to have our desires work for us. It is hard to find contentment in life because modern mentality puts so much emphasis on defining who we are by what we have, which of course, makes the very idea of not seeking possessions a foolish endeavor. Instead of thinking this way, we should consider Jesus who had nothing: was he worthless? If he was here today hanging out with the street bums, drug addicts, and sinners on the streets like he was in the days of old: what would we think? Would we go and listen to him or would we be too caught up in our world of desires and acquiring things?

When we get to this understanding, that yes, at this point in our lives we are not living up to our highest potential, that is when humbleness can begin to awaken within our hearts, and this awakening helps us overcome our spiritual grandeur and hubris. This humility is not the same as that which we find so often in modern Christian thought that conditions us to believe that we are hopeless and helpless. Jesus tells us in Matthew 16:24 to pick up our own cross and follow him. Does this sound like we are helpless? The humbleness we are seeking to embody is not rooted in such feeble thoughts, but comes from the awareness of our place in the Universe.

We all need help once in awhile. Even Jesus asked that the burden be lifted from him in Matthew 26:39. This type of powerlessness grants us strength and gives us the endurance and courage we need to carry on. It is at this point of utter humility that we come to realize what Jesus was talking about in Luke:

Behold, the Kingdom of God is within you. *(17:21)*

When we realize our true spiritual state a great sense of overwhelming abundance and everlasting peace arises within our hearts. This is when we inherit the Kingdom of GOD – for it has always been within us.

Things to contemplate

"Blessed are the poor in spirit: for theirs is the kingdom of heaven" (Matthew 5:3)
"Blessed be ye poor: for yours is the kingdom of God" (Luke 6:20)
- What does it mean to be poor in spirit?
- What is the difference between these two verses?
- What does "in spirit" mean?
- How do you feel about poor people?
- Why would being physically poor bless you?
- What is it about being rich that makes it so hard to get into heaven? (Matthew 19:24)
- Where do the Gospels support seeking worldly riches? Do not read anything from Paul – just the Four Gospels. When Jesus says that we should seek out riches, what is he talking about? (Matthew 13:22 & Matthew 6:20)
- What scriptural justifications have been used to seek out riches?
- How does being poor help you with faith and trusting in GOD? Likewise, does wealth bring about the same since of dependency and faith in GOD?

"Whosoever drinketh of this water shall thirst again. But, whosoever drinketh of the water that I shall give him shall never thirst; but the water that I shall give him shall be in him a well of water springing up into everlasting life." (John 4:13-14)
- What is this verse saying?
- What is the water? Is it liquid substance or something else?
- Why is water used to symbolize the teachings of Jesus?
- How is water important for life? What is the connection between the necessities of water for life and the teachings of Jesus?

"If ye were of the world, the world would love his own: but, because ye are not of the world, but I have chosen you out of the world, therefore the world hateth you." (John 15:19)
- What does "not of the world" mean?
- What does it mean "of the world"?
- Do you fit in with the world and its beliefs, systems, economies, politics, etc?

"Behold, the Kingdom of God is within you." (Luke 17:21)
- What is the Kingdom of GOD?
- How can the Kingdom be within you? Is it symbolic or maybe hinting at some mystical experience?
- What qualities would the Kingdom of GOD manifest?
- If you could bring heaven here on earth – what would that be like?

Practices to help you connect with this Beatitude

- Contemplate the never ending cycle of fulfilling your desires.
- Consider how comfortable you have become in your spirituality.
- Make a list of all the things you believe about the spirit. Take a moment to consider them? Do you really believe in these things or are they simply things you have adopted from others and habituated? What does it take for you to believe something? Do you simply believe in something or do you have to justify and validate your beliefs? Feelings, logic, and experiences are a few different ways beliefs are created. Which work for you?
- Consider how much energy (thinking, acting, desiring/dwelling) you spend towards physical well-being versus spiritual. Which one is more important? Are you one of those people who think you should get your physical well-being situated before moving towards spiritual practices? Does this fit with Matthew 6:31 which instructs us to not worry about what we will eat and drink, but rather to let the day take care of itself?

Mourn

> *Blessed are they that mourn: for they shall be comforted. (Matthew 5:4)*

How can comfort come from mourning? Anyone who has felt the genuine loss of something special knows that this feeling does not invite anything close to comfort. In fact, what it does bring is discomfort. Even so, one thing that comes close to comfort arises from the efforts of others who awkwardly try to relieve us of our loss with platitudes, and if possible, stories of their own losses in life. Another way loss can convey comfort is by bringing us closer to those we still have in our lives. This second aspect of comfort can in turn invite a genuine feeling of gratitude.

Unlike the material form of mourning that comes from physical loss, spiritual mourning arises when we begin to see how egocentric and ignorant we are: in other words, when we see how little we actually know about the Spirit, how conditioned our beliefs are, and how much we suffer for our self-centeredness. This awareness awakens a second form of mourning that we see in the story of the Prodigal Son. After losing everything, the son remembers and mourns for the great blessings of his father's house (Luke 15:11). Physically he recognizes his material losses: comfort, food, warmth, friends, family, and so on. Spiritually he recognizes how far he is from the Path; how his unquenchable desires have taken him away from himself and his true happiness.

The comfort that comes from mourning originates from the process of grieving itself. Grieving brings us in contact with some of our deepest fears and pains of life. We meet with loss; we travel for a while with death; we swim through confusion; we dance with fear, and in the end, if we can touch these things, open our hearts and breathe into them with our minds – it is that moment when we can truly let go and trust in GOD. When we are this vulnerable, when our egos, our knowledge, and everything else we hold onto so tightly falls away – that is when we truly touch GOD – that is when we find ourselves.

This does not get rid of the pain, it does not absolve the confusion nor replace what we have lost. What it does give us is awareness and compassion. When we can truly recognize the state of life, its impermanence, we learn to relax, we learn to let go, we learn to soften our fears that push us to cling with dear life to our desires and attachments. This unrecognized fear is so powerful, so dreadful, that we bury it deep within ourselves so that we do not have to face it. In burying it we fail to see just how powerful it is – how much it controls our lives. It's only when loss comes that we must face it. If we can confront it, if we can touch it, hold it, and let it go – there is no greater comfort than this.

Things to contemplate

"Blessed are they that mourn: for they shall be comforted." (Matthew 5:4)
- What does mourning mean? What is it?
- Have you mourned? Did you learn anything from the experience?
- How do you react to your surroundings while mourning? What about after?
- How do you deal and relate with those who are mourning?

Practices to help you connect with this Beatitude

- Make a list of ten things you have mourned over and ten things you would mourn over if you lost them today? Is there a connection between these two lists?
- Throughout the day contemplate the loss of those you care about. Experience the loss of them in a direct way. Then contemplate your death. What would you miss in life? Who would miss you? Think about these things: are you on good terms and do you appreciate those you care about?
- Randomly give up something you care about or do for yourself. Maybe skip the morning coffee, miss a meal, or not get something better than what you already have. These small sacrifices can help

you connect with those who do not have the resources or ability to do these things on their own. By denying yourself these things you can mentally send them to others – or better yet – you could actually make a point of getting and giving whatever you have denied yourself to others instead.

- Write a letter to all those you care about. Not an email or fax, but an actual letter with a stamp and envelope, and then send it. Even if this means sending it to your own partner or child – send the letter in the mail. Do not type it out either – write it by hand.

Meekness

Blessed are the meek: for they shall inherit the earth. (Matthew 5:5)

Humble and quiet, soft and gentle, open and receiving, trusting and supple: all these words help us understand what meekness is. Meekness tends to follow and be guided, and so those who are meek are those who give their wills and works to GOD. For meekness does not need to justify itself or shine above others as Jesus points out in Matthew:

He that is greatest among you shall be your servant. (23:11)

Only when we are humble and open can we receive the essence of the teachings:

> *Know this, my beloved brethren. Let every man be quick to hear, slow to speak, slow to anger, for the anger of man does not work the righteousness of God. Therefore put away all filthiness and rank growth of wickedness and receive with meekness the implanted word, which is able to save your souls. (James 1:19-21)*

If we think we know it all, how are we to learn? If we think we are pure, why would we want to become clean? If we think that we are healthy, why would we seek a physician? It is no wonder Jesus sought out those in lowly places, for they would never presume to place themselves above others:

I thank you, O Father, Lord of heaven and earth, because thou hast hid these things from the wise and prudent, and hast revealed them unto babes. (Matthew 11:25)

Just as a mouse who moves quietly in a house, gains everything of the house, so let us be meek in the world to inherit it.

Things to contemplate

"I thank you, O Father, Lord of heaven and earth, because thou hast hid these things from the wise and prudent, and hast revealed them unto babes." (Matthew 11:25)
- What things are hidden?
- What is this verse saying?
- Define what wise and prudent means.
- Which side are you on: babes or the wise? Be honest.

"Know this, my beloved brethren. Let every man be quick to hear, slow to speak, slow to anger, for the anger of man does not work the righteousness of God. Therefore put away all filthiness and rank growth of wickedness and receive with meekness the implanted word, which is able to save your souls." (James 1:19-21)
- "The anger of man does not work the righteousness of GOD." What does this mean?
- Is it possible to truly listen when you are just waiting to speak?
- Are you quick to speak or to listen?
- Can you really listen if you are angry?

"Blessed are the meek: for they shall inherit the earth." (Matthew 5:5)
- Define meekness?
- Do the meek really inherit anything? Think about the business world. How many CEOs, doctors, politicians, and lawyers do you think got there by being meek?
- What does "inherit the earth" mean?
- What does the earth represent?
- Do you consider yourself meek? Explain.

Practices to help you connect with this Beatitude

- Research history and find a saint or some religious figure and answer the following questions: What was their life like? Were they humble or aggressive, open or blocked, judgmental or accepting, giving or taking?
- Look at the life of Jesus and write down the ways he was meek. Did he come to rule or serve? How would you feel in his company?
- When in conversation stop trying to talk or waiting to talk and simply listen with the intent to hear what the other person is saying.
- Sit in an isolated space and have a conversation with Jesus. Tell him who you are. Do not be afraid – just spill your guts. If you do things that he might disagree with but you feel justified in doing them – argue your case with him. Tell him why you do the things you do, have the thoughts you have, or say the things you say. It is just you and him. No audience, no judge, no jury. Just your own justifications and the weight of the silent truth.

Hunger and Thirst

> **Blessed are they which do hunger and thirst after righteousness: for they shall be filled.** *(Matthew 5:6)*

Everything in the world disappears when we are hungry and thirsty – for there are few things more overwhelming than starvation. As we grow on the Christian Path we begin to feel a similar hunger, and this hunger directs us to cleave to Christ and righteousness as a newborn does to the bosom of its mother.

This insatiable hunger comes from the knowledge and understanding that nothing in this world can ever satisfy the great void within us. For the things of this world plague us and lead us down a never-ending cycle for anything that will satiate us. What we find on our journey is not some object of desire or some person in our dreams, but a humble teaching that guides us towards the Divine.

Righteousness in Matthew 5:6 is often interpreted as some form of external action, as if we are to go around the world correcting all the wrongs. If we look at the other seeds in this chapter we find that Jesus was talking about internal qualities to embody, not external qualities to enforce. In this regard we see that righteousness is not about eradicating other people's sins, but rather, overcoming our own:

> **Woe unto the world because of offenses! For it must needs be that offenses come; but woe to that man by whom the offenses cometh!** *(Matthew 18:7)*

The more righteous we become in action, thought, and speech the less fear, anxiety, worry, desire, anger, and confusion have over our lives. There is no greater freedom than to know that GOD or anyone else can witness what we are doing, saying, and thinking right at this moment or any moment, and not feel embarrassed, uncomfortable, or ashamed. This is what it means to be filled with peace and well-being – this is what it means to be righteous.

Things to contemplate

"Woe unto the world because of offenses! For it must needs be that offenses come; but woe to that man by whom the offenses cometh!" (Matthew 18:7)
- What is this verse pointing out?
- What do offenses mean?
- Why does this verse specify the one who does the offense and not the offense itself?

"Blessed are they which do hunger and thirst after righteousness: for they shall be filled." (Matthew 5:6)
- Define righteousness.
- What does it mean to hunger and thirst after righteousness?
- How can seeking for righteousness fill you?
- What are some signs of a righteous person?

Practices to help you connect with this Beatitude

- At random times during your day imagine someone watching your thoughts, speech, and actions and see if you would be okay with that.
- Make a list of all the righteous qualities of Jesus.
- Make a list of all the righteous qualities you wish to embody. Name some practices or actions you can do to bring you closer to them.

Merciful

Blessed are the merciful: for they shall obtain mercy. *(Matthew 5:7)*

True mercy comes from the deep understanding of our own miseries, mistakes, and losses. Being merciful and having mercy are two completely different things. The feeling of mercy comes from sympathy and pity. We see it most often come from those who have control and power over others. Being merciful on the other hand comes from a state of being filled with mercy (Mercy-full). It is a feeling that radiates from the heart. It does not evolve from pity, but from a deeply rooted feeling of compassion that arises when we have fully embraced our own suffering. Being merciful is a sign that we have gone to the depths of our being and returned whole.

When we can connect with our own faults and harmful thoughts, speech, and actions, the closer we are able to see clearly the sources of other people's suffering as the Good Samaritan in Luke 33 was able to do.

Things to contemplate

"Blessed are the merciful: for they shall obtain mercy" (Matthew 5:7).
- Define mercy.
- How can you obtain mercy by being merciful?
- What feelings arise when you feel merciful?

Practices to help you connect with this Beatitude

- Put yourself in other people's shoes.
- Make a list of all the things you feel pity or sorry for. Examples could be things like a mother with three children who has no support, caged animals, abused children, politicians in a pickle, etc... Once you come up with a few things, try to figure out why you feel this way.
- Make a list of things you wish to receive mercy for?
- Make a list of those you have not forgiven.
- What things do you hold onto – harbor?
- Go through the process of asking for forgiveness, forgiving, and letting go. Don't just think about it – do it!

Pure in heart

Blessed are the pure in heart: for they shall see GOD. (Matthew 5:8)

This is when our practices become real, authentic, and sincere. To be pure in heart is to have motivations that are always selfless and dedicated to GOD: there is neither falsehood nor egotism. When we have completely dedicated our whole life to the Christian Path, holding nothing back, only then can we touch upon this purity.

What does it take to be a Christian? Many of us believe that going to church and giving to some noble cause makes us a good Christian. We can do and say all the right things, and yet, have done nothing more than any other good person. The Path Jesus shared with us is not only about fellowship and giving, it is also about awakening the Christos through inner purifications and practices:

> *Cleanse first that which is within the cup and platter, that the outside of them may be clean also. (Matthew 23:26)*

The essence of this seed is self-awareness. By investigating our motivations and the origin of our thoughts we begin the process of unraveling the ego's chains. There are three signs of a person who has a pure heart: they never say or do anything that creates destructive suffering, their actions, speech, and thoughts open people's hearts rather than close them, and they never use guile, lies, manipulation, or force to accomplish things. Each sign points to a person who is aware of their actions and how their actions affect others. In other words, we could say that a person who exhibits these signs is GOD-centric not EGO-centric.

Things to contemplate

"Blessed are the pure in heart: for they shall see GOD." (Matthew 5:8)
- What does it mean to be pure at heart?
- What does it mean to see GOD?

"Cleanse first that which is within the cup and platter, that the outside of them may be clean also." (Matthew 23:26)
- What does it mean to cleanse the inside of the cup and platter?
- What needs to be cleansed?
- How can cleaning the inside make the outside clean?
- What connection is there between this verse and Matthew 15:8?

Practices to help you connect with this Beatitude

- Make a list of all your motivations for a week.
- See all living beings and things as part of GOD'S creation.
- Do the opposite of what you would normally do. For instance, maybe you have extra money that you were going to treat yourself with and then all of a sudden you cross paths with someone holding a sign on the off-ramp – instead of using that money for yourself, you give it away.
- Every time you sit down to meditate, study, or talk about something spiritual, dedicate it to GOD and to all of GOD'S creation.

Peacemakers

Blessed are the peacemakers: for they shall be called the children of GOD. (Matthew 5:9)

In Hebrew the word *Peace* is translated as wholeness. It could be loosely understood as a feeling of completeness and union with the Divine. This peace comes when we have stabilized our practices and begun the process of aligning ourselves with the teachings of Jesus. When we are impeccable we no longer need to look over our shoulder. There is nothing we have to hide, and in that state, there is no fear or worry.

There is godliness in those who have a pure heart and who are connected to GOD through right action, speech, and thought. Many believe that this is not possible – but why would Jesus tell us to do something impossible (Matthew 5:48). It is not easy, but it is possible, and it all starts by hungering and thirsting for it.

This leads us to better understand what a peacemaker is. They have found this wholeness and peace within themselves, and this peace radiates from them like a light from a flame. These children of GOD emit light for all to see by. They are the saints and godly people of the past and present who have completely given themselves over to the Path.

Sometimes we mistake someone who is striving to keep the peace with a peacemaker. Although keeping the peace is a noble act, it is not always the right action to take. We can look back in history and see that some of the noblest and peaceful people had to stand up against aggression and ignorance. Three examples are Jesus when he entered the temple and threw all the merchants out, Gandhi in India, and Martin Luther King in America. A peacemaker is a person who is a living embodiment of the truth. They might have to stand up to ignorance and aggression. They might have to fight, turn over tables, stand up against injustices. The difference is, they do it with a heart filled with love and deep understanding that comes from the spring of blessedness. This spring wells up within us when the Seeds of Christ have borne their fruits. When we have reached this point we can see how it is possible to love even our enemies:

> *Love your enemies, bless them that curse you, do good to them that hate you, and pray for them which despitefully use you, and persecute you.* (Matthew 5:44)

This is hard to swallow when we look from our modern state of mind. Why would we seek to do good things for those who wish us harm?

Things to contemplate

"Blessed are the peacemakers: for they shall be called the children of GOD." (Matthew 5:9)
- Define peace and peacemaker.
- Why would a peacemaker be called a child of GOD?
- Would someone who creates war be called a peacemaker? Why or why not?

"Love your enemies, bless them that curse you, do good to them that hate you, and pray for them which despitefully use you, and persecute you." (Matthew 5:44)
- What is this verse saying?
- Do you practice this? Explain why or why not.
- What do you think would come about if you practice this?

Practices to help you connect with this Beatitude

- Four degrees of action:
    1. Acting out of fear.
    2. Acting out of desire.
    3. Acting for a reward. (Do unto others as we wish them to do unto us).
    4. Acting for action's sake.
- By doing righteous things to the least of your brethren you do it to Jesus also. Do you believe this?
- Talk through issues instead of burying them.

- Think of one thing you feel really strongly about, then research the opposite viewpoint. Write a paper arguing the opposing view until you reach a point when either your way or the other could feasibly be accepted as truth.
- When an argument or disagreement arises, take a second to breathe in with the intention of gaining a larger perspective. Look in the other person's eye and say to yourself, "they feel as strongly as I do." Think of how you would want them to talk to you. Send them love and understanding before proceeding.
- Try to hear what people are really saying. Are they feeling hurt, attacked, etc?
- When someone offends or verbally attacks, simply use the opportunity to send love – because that is what they need.
- Make a list of all the people you hate, dislike, mistrust, or fear and give reasons why you feel this way about them.

Persecuted

> ***Blessed are they which are persecuted for righteousness' sake: for theirs is the Kingdom of Heaven.*** *(Matthew 5:10)*

This verse teaches us to let go, trust, be patient, selfless, open, and humble. The first Beatitude teaches us humility and contentment, this one puts it to the test. In fact, this Beatitude tests, refines, and perfects them all.

One thing we need to keep in mind is that these teachings are not trying to create suffering in our lives. For instance, this verse is not telling us to go out and get persecuted for being righteous, or to meditate until we manifest suffering. What it is saying is that it happens. When we live in accordance with the teachings of Jesus, it has a tendency to reflect back to others their weaknesses and ignorance. Suffering likes company, but it does not like to look at itself, and so, by living in the way's of Christ we will make enemies. Most people are not ready to change and grow. Our dearest friends, church members, and even our families will turn against us because of it.

> **Brother shall deliver up brother to death, and the father the child: and the children shall rise up against their parents and cause them to be put to death. And ye shall be hated of all men for my name's sake: but he that endureth to the end shall be saved.** *(Matthew 10:21-22)*

A morbid picture for sure, but it gets to the point. This verse reminds us that the Kingdom of Heaven is ours if we plant these seeds. This verse supports and reminds us that we are doing the right thing. Although the whole world might be against us, if we are living in accordance with these and similar teachings, we are walking The Narrow Path. If we are humble, constantly striving towards compassion and peace, open and receptive, dedicating every moment to the Path, completely aware of our motivations, and always trying to keep our lives and all of life in balance, then we are creating the Kingdom of Heaven here on earth. Why wait for heaven after death when we can bring Divine blessings into the world through our lives today.

Things to contemplate

"Blessed are they which are persecuted for righteousness' sake: for theirs is the Kingdom of Heaven." (Matthew 5:10)
- What does persecuted mean?
- How could you be blessed for being persecuted?
- What is the difference between being persecuted for beliefs versus being persecuted for righteous actions?
- Why would someone be persecuted for being righteous?
- How could being righteous become a vice? Think about the ego when answering this.

"Brother shall deliver up brother to death, and the father the child: and the children shall rise up against their parents and cause them to be put to death. And ye shall be hated of all men for my name's sake: but he that endureth to the end shall be saved." (Matthew 10:21-22)
- What is this verse saying?
- Do you see less dramatic ways this verse plays out in life?

- What does it mean to endure till the end?
- What is the end? Is it some apocalyptic ending or simply the transition of death? Are they the same thing?

Practices to help you connect with this Beatitude

- The first thing you can do is take an unwanted situation as a chance to practice being patient, open, loving, understanding, aware, forgiving, and so on. It is not easy to turn an unwanted moment into a chance for practice, but by desiring to transform unwanted situations into an opportunity to practice is key to transforming yourself and awakening the qualities of Christ within.
- After the situation has gone or the energy has dispersed you can begin to ask these and similar questions: are they speaking truth, is there something you are hiding from yourself, was fear and anger involved, were you being egotistical, a know-it-all, et cetera? By asking these and similar questions you gain a great opportunity to learn and grow.
- The last thing you can do is grow from the experience. How did you deal with the situation, what can you do in the future, how were you feeling, what kind of thoughts were arising, were you being judgmental, closing down, etc. After going through the many questions that can arise then plan for the future by saying things like: in the future I will be more open, in the future I will pay more attention to others needs, in the future I will breathe and think before I speak, and so on. By doing this you are helping yourself be in the moment rather than react to the emotions and thoughts that arise from defensiveness, hurt, anger, and all the other harmful emotions and thoughts that arise within.

Connecting the Beatitudes

What ties all these seeds together? The most obvious answer is that each practice blesses us in one way or another. The second thing is that the first and last Beatitudes promise the Kingdom of Heaven. These two verses bind all the Beatitudes together. The first Beatitude tells us that by embodying these inner qualities we gain the Kingdom of Heaven, while the last

Beatitude reminds us to stay our course through thick and thin for the Kingdom.

The first three Beatitudes address the inner qualities that help us sever our old ways and become reborn as children of GOD. Many people look at these first three Beatitudes as negative or unnecessarily dark in nature because they focus on pain, suffering, and sadness. While this is the case, the intention is to help us break through ignorance, attachments, and our old ways of reacting to life. As we enter into the fourth Beatitude we have gained the strength and insight to direct ourselves towards embodying the righteous qualities of Christ. This search for righteousness leads us to become merciful, pure, and peaceful. The first four Beatitudes point at our current state of being, the last four Beatitudes point to a state of being that we can embody through prayer and practice.

Each seed brings us closer to GOD. First is the promise that we will gain the Kingdom, next we are comforted from our troubles, before gaining the blessings of connecting with GOD through creation and being filled with GOD'S blessings by striving towards righteousness. After being filled we receive mercy and peace from our troubles before coming to see GOD through purity. As our journey continues we become children of GOD, and then, as was promised from the beginning, we enter into the Kingdom of Heaven – awakening the Divine within us.

These are the seeds we grow in our lives. They are the core teachings of Jesus. Throughout this text we will always come back to them to see where we are at on our journey. As i have said and will always say, the Path of Christianity is not easy. It is not something we do on the weekend when we have some extra time on our hands and need to atone for the things that we have done. Being a Christian is something we live moment to moment. When we say we are a Christian, we are saying that we embody these things – for being a Christian is to have awakened the Christos within. Otherwise, all that we can say is that we are trying to follow in the footsteps of Jesus.

Chapter Three
Rooting the Mind

- Being Focused
- Being Content
- Being free of Jealousy
- Being free of Judgment
- Being free of Expectations
- Being Joyful
- Being Sacred

While the Seeds of Christ in section two show us what to strive towards and embody, the following practices help us develop the right type of thinking we need to have on the Path.

Without focus it is very difficult to accomplish our aims. When we are not content the world becomes a battle ground we must always fight for or against. Jealousy tears at our hearts and minds, judgment separates us from GOD's creation, and having expectations constantly unbalances us. Being joyful and recognizing the sacredness of life is what really helps us work through our issues so that we can awaken the Christos in our lives.

Being Focused

> *The light of the body is the eye: if therefore thine eye be single, thy whole body shall be full of light.*
> *(Matthew 6:22)*

Without focus there is no direction, when there is no direction there is no Path. When we keep our minds focused on the Path of Christ all our actions, words, and thoughts move towards truth, wisdom, and peace. It is our intentions that build the energy necessary to keep our feet treading this hard and difficult Path. This focus is like the mother whom constantly has her eyes on her children while doing everything she always does. She can be doing the dishes, hanging up clothes, or anything else, and the moment her child is in danger, she feels it and goes to protect the child before it gets hurt. Just because we are focused on the Path does not mean we turn away from life. What happens instead is that our lives become the Path.

Descartes said, "I think, therefore I am." While we know there is more to us then just our thoughts, what he was hinting at leads us to a great secret. Instead of our thoughts validating our existence, we can conceive of them as defining our existence. In other words, we are what we think just as much as what we eat. When we focus whole heartily on the teachings of Jesus, our bodies and minds begin to shift and become more Christ-like. All it takes for us to begin walking the Path is to have the focus, intention, and will to walk with Jesus, and it will happen.

When the mind is unfocused many things can interfere with our walk: distractions come like uninvited guests. The longer our minds remain untethered, the less control we have over them. We might think we have control because we can create a similitude of balance within our lives. But what we find in life is that it only takes a thief, a natural disaster, or some other thing to turn our world upside down. The only two things we can truly control in life are our thoughts and reactions to the stimuli in our lives. When we are focused and intentional we gain some control over these two things. It is not something that we can do for a while and then slack off as the story of the demon returning to the house in Matthew 12:43-45 points out. It is a practice that we must always remain vigilant with just like the brides waiting for the groom in Matthew 25:1-12.

Things to contemplate

"The light of the body is the eye: if therefore thine eye be single, thy whole body shall be full of light." (Matthew 6:22)
- What does it mean the "light of the body is the eye?"
- What does "single" mean?

- How can you keep your eye single?
- How can keeping the eye single make your whole body "full of light?"
- What does "full of light" mean?

Practices to help invite focus

- Make a list of your top intentions in life.
- Constantly bring the mind to your practices.
- Always contemplate a verse or bring verses into your day to invite insight, encouragement, and appreciation.
- Work on awareness practices. Some different things you can use to bring awareness into your life are to focus and meditate with any of these things:
    a. Bodily sensations
    b. Emotions
    c. Thoughts
    d. Experiences
    e. Conversations
    f. Intentions and motivations
    g. Desires and wants
    h. Whatever you are doing right now

Being Content

> *Godliness with contentment is great gain. For we brought nothing into this world, and it is certain that we will carry nothing out. And having food and raiment, let us be therewith content. But they that will be rich fall into temptation and a snare, and into many foolish and hurtful lusts, which drown men in destruction and perdition. For the love of money is the root of all evil: which while some coveted after, they have erred from the faith, and pierced themselves through with many sorrows. (1 Timothy 6:6-10)*

The source of our greatest peace and worst suffering comes from the abundance or lack of contentment in our lives. It is believed by many that life is about being happy and joyful. If this is true, then why is there so much suffering in life? Even those who see life as perfect or who have all the money in the world to spend have a difficult time attaining this joy and happiness. So the question remains, "Why is there so much pain, loss, and misery in the world when all we want is happiness?" The only answer that makes since to me is that we are either looking for the wrong thing or going about it in the wrong way.

When we see our happiness and joy slipping away, that is when we can begin to figure out where we are going wrong. We all want to be happy – but for some reason most of us have a hard time finding lasting happiness. When we seek happiness through controlling life, we often find ourselves disappointed as life falls apart around us. When we seek happiness in material things, we are again dumbfounded as we watch our happiness disappears with the objects of our desire. If on the other hand we base our happiness on relationships and family, we once again find the illusive happiness and joy slipping through our fingers as life's circumstances come knocking on our door.

If all these things we struggle to gain and keep are not the essence of life's happiness, then what is? The answer does not come to us through reason, it comes to us through the examples of those who have found it. When we look to them we see their happiness, peace, and joy not arising from some object or dream, but from being content with life as it is. They do not have to strive for material possessions, make friends, or expect the world to be anything other than what it is. Each and every one of them lives with what is before them.

What is it like when we get exactly what we want? At that moment we have it all: the whole world seems to be going our way. Everything is brighter, sharper, and more beautiful. But what happens to that feeling? If it is so great, why does it disappear? Of course, we have many desires, so there is no one desire that will fulfill us, but why does it not at least continue to give us a feeling of contentment? No matter how hard we try to find fulfillment, there will always be something else we will want. We can spend our whole life acquiring things and never have the fulfillment that we seek.

> *The Kingdom of Heaven is like unto a man that is a householder, which went out early in the morning to hire laborers into his vineyard. And when he had agreed with the laborers for a penny a day he sent them into his vineyard. And he went out about the third hour, and saw others standing idle in the marketplace. And said unto them; "Go ye also into the vineyard, and whatsoever is right I will give unto you." And they went their way. Again about the eleventh hour he went out, and found others standing idle, and saith unto them, 'Why stand ye here all the day idle?' They say unto him, 'Because no man hath hired us.' He saith unto them, 'Go ye also into the vineyard and whatsoever is right, that shall ye receive.' So when evening was come, the lord of the vineyard saith unto his steward, 'Call the laborers, and give them their hire, beginning from the last unto the first.' And when they came that were hired about the eleventh hour, they received every man a penny. But when the first came, they supposed that they should have received more; and they likewise received every man a penny. And when they had received it, they murmured against the Goodman of the house. Saying, 'These last have wrought but one hour, and thou hast made them equal unto us, which have borne the burden and heat of the day.' But he answered one of them and said, 'Friend, I do thee no wrong: didst not thou agree with me for a penny? Take that thine is, and go thy way.' (Matthew 20:1-3)*

A big part of discontent comes when we compare ourselves with others. We look to others and see their happiness and contentment and so we want what they have. If only we could stop for a moment and look at them closely we would see that they are playing the same game as well. There is nothing wrong with enjoying the simple things in life – from the basic amenities to the extra things like televisions, computers, radios, vacations, fruit juicers, or whatever. All these things are good for freeing up time, making life simpler or easier, bringing enjoyment and pleasure into our lives, and expanding our imagination and understanding. The problem is not the thing, but the lust, hunger, and desire which fills our minds for them. When the love for money, prestige, honor, and possessions become the meaning and reason for life, then life has been replaced by an illusion that takes us away from itself.

There is always a belief that this thing, person, place, or dream will fulfill us. If that were true, then why are we still striving and searching? Who is the one holding the carrot?

Things to contemplate

"Godliness with contentment is great gain. For we brought nothing into this world, and it is certain that we will carry nothing out. And having food and raiment, let us be therewith content. But they that will be rich fall into temptation and a snare, and into many foolish and hurtful lusts, which drown men in destruction and perdition. For the love of money is the root of all evil: which while some coveted after, they have erred from the faith, and pierced themselves through with many sorrows." (1Timothy 6:6-10)

- Define contentment.
- What would it take for you to be content?
- Why does it say the "love of money is the root of all evil" and not money itself?
- How does the desire to retire at 55 or so fit in with this verse?
- What one thing in your life gives you contentment ALL the time? Is it music – then listen to it non-stop for three days and see what happens. Is it food – then eat and eat and eat and see how you feel after awhile. Is it sex – then why not have it all the time - why would you ever want to stop? Is it children – really? All the time? The idea of this exercise is to show that there is no tangible thing in this world that invites everlasting contentment.

"The Kingdom of Heaven is like unto a man that is a householder, which went out early in the morning to hire laborers into his vineyard. And when he had agreed with the laborers for a penny a day he sent them into his vineyard. And he went out about the third hour, and saw others standing idle in the marketplace. And said unto them; "Go ye also into the vineyard, and whatsoever is right I will give unto you." And they went their way. Again about the eleventh hour he went out, and found others standing idle, and saith unto them, "Why stand ye here all the day idle?" They say unto him, "Because no man

hath hired us." He saith unto them, "Go ye also into the vineyard and whatsoever is right, that shall ye receive." So when evening was come, the lord of the vineyard saith unto his steward, "Call the laborers, and give them their hire, beginning from the last unto the first." And when they came that were hired about the eleventh hour, they received every man a penny. But when the first came, they supposed that they should have received more; and they likewise received every man a penny. And when they had received it, they murmured against the Goodman of the house. Saying, "These last have wrought but one hour, and thou hast made them equal unto us, which have bourn the burden and heat of the day." But he answered one of them and said, "Friend, I do thee no wrong: didst not thou agree with me for a penny? Take that thine is, and go thy way." (Matthew 20:1-3)

- What does this verse teach you about contentment?
- Why does contentment disappear as soon as you compare yourself with others?
- Name someone you know who is really content? A neighbor, family member, lawyer, preacher, church member? Anybody? If you can bring yourself to do it, go ask them if they are really content. If you find them to be truly content, ask them how they do it and listen to their answer! It is possible.

Practices to help invite contentment

- How does ruminating on the past and fantasying about the future keep you away from contentment? For one day really try to avoid getting caught up in the past or future and try instead to bring your mind to what is before you and be grateful.
- Go back in your memory and find a place where the desire you are currently stuck with did not exist. Did you exist? Was your life unbearable? Did your life lack meaning? What changed? How does desire deplete life?
- Make a list of all the things you are grateful for: parts of the body, hobbies, people, experiences, foods, drugs, and whatever else you can think of. Keep adding to this list for the rest of your life.
- Meditate on how your expectations create suffering in your life when they are not fulfilled.
- How much time do you spend working towards physical possessions? What about spiritual qualities? What does that say about your priorities? Do you think that once you have gotten all the physical needs and desires fulfilled that you will then be able to focus more on spiritual things? Can desire itself really be fulfilled? What happens if you die before that day? Would your life be worth it? Would you have any regrets?

Being free of Jealousy

> *For ye are yet carnal: for whereas there is among you envying, strife, and divisions, are ye not carnal, and walk as me.* (1 Corinthians 3:3)

Jealousy is one of the harshest and deepest emotions that arise in our lives. It comes from seeing what another has and what we lack or from a fear that grows in our relationships. There are many facets of jealousy, each of which reflect a feeling of inadequacy that inevitably leads to fear and anger: fear of losing or not gaining something and anger to protect us when we are vulnerable.

The antidotes for jealousy are trust, goodwill, and letting go of attachments, desires, and expectations. When we trust it helps keep our minds open to seeing things for what they really are. Of course, sometimes our partner might very well be having relations with another person. As sad as this is, it does happen. When we can keep our minds open in these situations we find that the unfolding of the relationship, be it a separation or re-awakening of the bond, is done with a mind that remains clear and unfettered to those sticky emotions that tear at our hearts and corrupt our minds.

Goodwill comes from the deepest feeling of love within us. It seeks to bring happiness into the world rather than hoard it. Even in our most hurtful relationships we can choose to send love rather than hatred and anger. This might be hard, especially when it affects our relationships with friends and family, our living situation, our employment, and our children. The choices we have though are either jealousy, which creates a lot of tension and negativity, or we can wish them great happiness in their endeavors and pray that our hearts remain open as we go through the transition. The latter response does not get back at the other person; there is no feeling of justified revenge, and because of that, this practice is very difficult to do when we are hurt. But if we can bring ourselves to do it: something happens – the love remains even though the trust might not. And this love, rather than turning into hatred, becomes a bridge for more love to enter into our lives. This goodwill also applies to the jealousy that arises when we see other people's fortune. When we can bless others, we open ourselves to receive blessings in return.

The last antidote for jealousy is letting go. If we have taken these teachings seriously and begun to practice, then we have already begun to let go. The more we practice, the less jealousy will appear in our lives. When we can really let go of our expectations and desires, the chance of jealousy entering into our lives is minimized, if not eradicated – for there is no root from which jealousy can grow as we are told in Romans:

> *Let us walk honestly, as in the day; not in rioting and drunkenness, not in chambering and wantonness, not in strife and envying. (13:13)*

Things to contemplate

"For ye are yet carnal: for whereas there is among you envying, strife, and divisions, are ye not carnal, and walk as me." (1 Corinthians 3:3)
- Define carnal?
- Why are we carnal when we are jealous?
- Contemplate and define the word jealousy (Jail – Lousy). Being imprisoned by misery.
- How does jealousy keep us away from contentment?
- Make a list of all the things in your life that invite jealousy?

"Let us walk honestly, as in the day; not in rioting and drunkenness, not in chambering and wantonness, not in strife and envying" (Romans 13:13)
- What does it mean walking "honestly, as in the day?" What connection does this verse have with being Pure in Heart?
- What does this verse tell us about jealousy?
- Have you ever been jealous? If so, what was it like? How did the world appear to you? Were you happy? What did you learn?

Practices to help overcome jealousy

- Have trust and when you do not feel trust, take a moment to look at what is happening in your mind – why can't you trust?
- Have good will towards others by sending them love, abundance, and joy.
- Continue working on letting go. Give away the moment of stress, distrust, jealousy, and selfishness.
- Change the storyline. In this practice you transform the way you see things by literally changing the thoughts that support jealousy. In this case you can look from a third person perspective and see how your story unfolds from an objective observer's point of view. As you do this you can change the story without being attached to the feelings. Then when you enter into the story with the new narrative and experience the feelings and thoughts that arise from this new perspective, it becomes easier to deal with the situation as it unfolds in your life.
- Work with the feelings and transforming them with the compassion practice in chapter seven.
- Confronting and communicating with the other person or situation that's triggering jealousy instead of allowing the mind to go through a zillions scenarios of what might or might not actually be happening. Being truthful with your feelings and thoughts can often lead you towards a path of freedom.
- Trace the source of jealousy. Not the situation that has triggered it, but that vulnerable and hurtful place. Use this moment to dive into the depths of your being – feel the agonizing pain and then let it go.

Being free of Judgment

> *He that is without sin among you, let him first cast a stone at her.* (John 8:7)

Why do we judge when Jesus tells us, "Judge not, that ye be not judged" (Matthew 7:1)? It is a natural adaptation of life to discern what is harmful, beneficial, or neutral to our physical and emotional well-being. It is our human lot to attach aversion (bad), desire (good), or indifference (insignificance) to those things. That is when discernment becomes a judgment. This added mental substance is what separates us from the world we live in.

We walk a fine line when we play the judging game. The safest path to take is to let go of our concepts of what we think and believe is right or wrong and leave it to GOD to "sift between the tares and the wheat" (Matthew 13:24-30). We might be justified in our judgments, but there is always the chance that our thoughts could mislead us. Instead of weeding out the truth, we might cause harm to someone or something instead.

One misunderstanding that arises when we let go of our judgments is that somehow we will be allowing people and situations to cause us harm with no consequence – that by withholding judgment we are somehow excusing the behavior or situation. What protects us from this are the laws put into place to create a harmonious society. When we choose to murder or steal, we choose consciously or unconsciously to suffer the consequences of our actions. The difference between the laws of the land and the judgments that happen within our mind regarding those things we like or dislike, is the effect they have on our mental state. One helps balance a situation, the other separates us from it. Below is an example of how judgments can affect our relationship with the world.

A person is arrested for brutally murdering another person. Many will feel pity for the murdered person and indignation or outright hatred towards the murderer. Later we find out that the murderer was a father protecting his child from being kidnapped. Maybe our initial judgment was unfairly projected into the situation and now seeing a bigger picture we start to feel remorse and sympathy for the father. As the trial unfolds we get the complete story. It turns out that the real criminal was the stepfather who on the behest of the mother, attempted to kidnap her son and in the process killed the child's biological father who had legal custody.

Our minds are clouded by judgments which make it hard for us to see the bigger picture. This cloudiness keeps us from experiencing life directly. As Jesus points out in Matthew, "cast out the beam out of thine own eye; and then shalt thou see clearly to cast out the mote out of thy brother's eye" (7:5).

As we watch our minds we learn just how much time we spend judging everything around us. This judging mind distances us from life. We categorize and label everything into neat and safe drawers in the hopes of feeling secure. What we find as we do this is that something as simple as seeing a tree and calling it, "Just a tree," is one of the many ways our minds separates us from the beauty of life. The fact that not one leaf will ever be the same on any other tree forever simply escapes us as commonplace. We judge color, sound, smell, sight, touch, thought, and whatever else we can grasp upon – and for that matter – even those things we cannot grasp or understand. Every one of our judgments separate us from the world we live in: that's out there and I am in here. Such judgments define what can bring happiness into our lives and what creates misery. All of it is simply a projection of what we want or do not want in our lives.

Another form of judgment is self-judgment. One kind of self-judgment arise from thoughts like: I don't deserve it, who am I, I am not doing it right or not trying hard enough, I am stupid, and so forth. Still another form of self-judgment is the gratifying type: I am the best, look at me, how great I am, and on and on. Most agree that the first kind of self-judgments are harmful to us while the second type of self-judgments are beneficial. But even the affirming judgments have a way of creating separation and eventually sorrow. While thoughts like, "I am the best or I am doing great" might seem to be beneficial, over time they collapse on themselves and become just like the first type of self-judgment. We justify affirming judgments because we believe they will make us better and stronger, but when we get to their essence, they separate us from the world just as much as the first type.

When we become aware of our judgments we gain a great opportunity to transform ourselves. It's difficult to change the flow and substance of our thoughts. Once we begin this process it gets even worse. While before we were unaware of all the thoughts and judgments that flowed through us, now that we are our world becomes chaotic: everything is colored by our judgments. Instead of lessening, our judgments become deafening. No wonder lasting happiness eludes us. Over time, and this can be a very long time, our judging minds start to relax, soften, and clear. Judgments begin to lighten and become translucent. As we continue to work on ourselves the coarse thoughts disappear and subtle ones arise. These subtle judgments distort our lives in little ways. At this level it is only through persistent practice and patience that we can let them go and enter into a place of complete and total freedom from judgments – a place of pure being.

Things to contemplate

"He that is without sin among you, let him first cast a stone at her." (John 8:7)
- Define sin.
- What is the origination of sin?
- Does throwing the first stone apply only to those that have committed that particular sin or does it mean any sin?
- Create an acronym for sin. Example: (S)eparation, (I)gnorance, (N)egativity

Practices to help let go of judgments

- Investigate how judgments separate you from others.
- Make a list of all the things that you hate when you are angry.
- Write about the different levels of judging.
- List twenty things you judge frequently in life.
- For one week write down everything you judge.
- Analyze your judgments and see if you agree with them.
- What effect does judging have on your life?
- Consider how judgments cause you harm. For instance, missing opportunities, building relationships, draining you through obsession and habituation, taking you away from the present moment, et cetera.

- Will yourself to stop judging. Build your will with the desire to stop judging. Use reason to strengthen desire.
- Watch your mind incessantly.

Being free of Expectations

> *For the kingdom of heaven is like unto a man that is an householder, which went out early in the morning to hire labourers into his vineyard.And when he had agreed with the labourers for a penny a day, he sent them into his vineyard.And he went out about the third hour, and saw others standing idle in the marketplace,And said unto them; Go ye also into the vineyard, and whatsoever is right I will give you. And they went their way.Again he went out about the sixth and ninth hour, and did likewise.And about the eleventh hour he went out, and found others standing idle, and saith unto them, Why stand ye here all the day idle?They say unto him, Because no man hath hired us. He saith unto them, Go ye also into the vineyard; and whatsoever is right, that shall ye receive.So when even was come, the lord of the vineyard saith unto his steward, Call the labourers, and give them their hire, beginning from the last unto the first.And when they came that were hired about the eleventh hour, they received every man a penny.But when the first came, they supposed that they should have received more; and they likewise received every man a penny. And when they had received it, they murmured against the goodman of the house, Saying, These last have wrought but one hour, and thou hast made them equal unto us, which have borne the burden and heat of the day.But he answered one of them, and said, Friend, I do thee no wrong: didst not thou agree with me for a penny?*
> *(Matthew 20:1-13)*

There is a subtle shift in our lives when we stop focusing on what we will get and what should be, and instead focus on what is: "I will be paid, they will owe me one, do unto others as we wish them to do unto us, I will go to heaven, I will gain great honor, they should be like this or do that, etc..." When we stop focusing on what ought to be and instead focus on what we are doing and what is really going on, a weight is lifted from our shoulders. Instead of basing our happiness and peace on our expectation being fulfilled we find happiness in what's before us and what we are doing. There is no contingency – there is no trade off – there's just life and living it.

There is a vast difference between those who do things for selfish reason and who expect the world to be a certain way and those who do things with no thought of reward, desire, or expectation. When we act for a reward our actions become colored by that reward. If we are paid by the hour we might stretch a job out, rush a job if we are paid for the job, and take short cuts, buy cheaper material, or possibly leave things undone if we feel we are not getting paid enough. On the other hand, those who labor for the sake of working and doing things with no expectations, they would never take shortcuts or do things shabbily. The work is the reward, and so, we seek perfection in the work itself. As contradictory as it might seem, when we are fully present with what is without expectations and desires we end up getting exactly what we need to be happy and be taken care of.

> *Be not therefore like unto them: for your Father knoweth what things ye have need of before ye ask him.* (Matthew 6:8)

This is a very hard practice because it strikes directly at our selfish nature. It is completely natural in the animal kingdom to seek out own interest, yet Jesus teaches us to go beyond the norm when he tells us to strive for perfection.

When we are able to act with no desire for reward, acknowledgement, or honor, we find our actions becoming more spontaneous, open, authentic, and joyful. We no longer act from the place of expectation but from a place of openness and awe as we witness the Spirit awaken within us.

Of course a householder must take care of their family, and so, they cannot work for nothing. The truth is, we need money to survive in society. The key is to let go of our expectations, hopes, and desires as the story of the workers in the field teach us above. Once we find employment that we agree with and whose given wages are something we can accept, we can then let go of our attachments and desires and dedicate our lives to the Path. It should not matter after the fact that maybe someone is working half as hard and getting paid the same or working half the time and getting paid more. The point is that we happily agreed to work for the given wages and it should not matter what other people are doing or making. If we trust, if we are open, if we joyfully embrace the moment, if we work hard and have little desire, things have a way of balancing out. In fact, the less desire and expectations we have, the greater our contentment – the greater our contentment – the greater our happiness.

Things to contemplate

"For the kingdom of heaven is like unto a man that is an householder, which went out early in the morning to hire labourers into his vineyard.And when he had agreed with the labourers for a penny a day, he sent them into his vineyard.And he went out about the third hour, and saw others standing idle in the marketplace,And said unto them; Go ye also into the vineyard, and whatsoever is right I will give you. And they went their way.Again he went out about the sixth and ninth hour, and did likewise.And about the eleventh hour he went out, and found others standing idle, and saith unto them, Why stand ye here all the day idle?They say unto him, Because no man hath hired us. He saith unto them, Go ye also into the vineyard; and whatsoever is right, that shall ye receive.So when even was come, the lord of the vineyard saith unto his steward, Call the labourers, and give them their hire, beginning from the last unto the first.And when they came that were hired about the eleventh hour, they received every man a penny.But when the first came, they supposed that they should have received more; and they likewise received every man a penny. And when they had received it, they murmured against the goodman of the house, Saying, These last have wrought but one hour, and thou hast made them equal unto us, which have borne the burden and heat of the day.But he answered one of them, and said, Friend, I do thee no wrong: didst not thou agree with me for a penny?" (Matthew 20:1-13).

- What is this verse saying?

Rooting the Mind   69

- If the workers who started in the morning were paid first, how might their feelings change? Why?
- How do expectations invite discontent?
- Do expectations make you happy?
- Are expectations good? Explain.

Practices to help let go of expectations

- Write down all the times you have done something without wanting a reward. This includes not expecting gratitude or thanks.
- What do you expect from GOD?
- Make a list of different actions that have no desire for result.
- Purposely create situations where the opportunity to give arises without the need for gratitude. What were the results? Did you end up expecting something? What were your thoughts and feelings?
- Start to investigate how expectations effect/affect you? What happens when your expectations are met? What about when they are not? How often are your expectations met?
- While this section deals primarily with the expectations that arise from doing things, how might your expectations of others affect your experiences in life? Recognize that while expectations can often be productive and encouraging, they can also be detrimental and harmful. Look at both sides of the coin.

Being Joyful

Rejoice in the Lord always: and again I say, Rejoice. (Philippians 4:4)

One misconception that arises from this practice is the idea that we always have to be happy. A big part of following in the footsteps of Jesus is to be authentic. He showed fear and doubt, anger and frustration, and still was able to see the great blessings of life in the midst of persecution. The idea of always having a joyful mind is not about pretending to be happy when we are sad or angry, or to ignore the suffering in life while trying to keep the mind on some utopian ideal. It is about inviting a certain state of being that looks through the lens of life's blessings rather than through the lens of suffering. To have a joyful mind is to have a mind that remains open to every situation that comes up. The mind does not judge bad or good, it merely remains open and seeks to grow from the lessons that each situation has to offer.

When we have a joyful mind – life is beautiful. It might be hard and filled with suffering, but it is not bad or evil. We are all given many opportunities in life. Some of us might have horrible situations and live in the worst conditions, and the possibility of finding a joyful mind is very hard to achieve. Even so, we can still try to awaken joyfulness in our lives by having our hearts open to the world and the things that come our way. When we are able to do that, we come to understand what Jesus meant when he tells us to "knock and it shall be open, ask and you will receive" (Matthew 7:7). When we seek to invite joyfulness into our lives – it comes.

Life is not powered by greed or selfishness – it is powered by the energy it takes to create a joy filled heart and mind. Always having a joyful mind creates a space within and around us that turns the night into day and pain into a practice that we can grow from instead of running away from and fighting against. Pain and suffering are a part of life, but so is joyfulness and bliss. When we invite joyfulness into our lives, everything in our life opens to joyfulness: even pain and suffering.

Life is a beautiful place. There are many horrible things in this world, but there are also many beautiful things. Some of the greatest things in life are those rare moments when we connect with nature or with another living being. The idea behind having a joyful mind is that we become open to everything. By becoming open, we find ourselves connecting with those rare moments of boundless joy more often.

Being joyful is not about pretending to be happy or trying to control reality with our minds, it's simply an open-ended way of perceiving life without getting caught up in the clinging nature of the ego's desire to control and solidify reality. With this practice we are merely trying to open our hearts to life and find joy in all our experiences – even the bad ones. How are we to find joy when we are in pain, being robbed, raped, yelled at, and a host of other crappy situations? There is no easy answer. The fact is, while in the mist of any of these things, joy is far away. Life sucks sometimes – there is no way of getting around that. The key is to try. Try to find the joy, the abundance, the moment of freshness when life just is. When we are caught up in the past or grasping for the future – joy cannot be. Finding the present moment – that is the key.

Things to contemplate

"Rejoice in the Lord always: and again I say, Rejoice." (Philippians 4:4)
- What is joy?
- How is joy connected to giving thanks?
- Write a list of all the things that invite joy in your life.
- Why is rejoicing so important?
- How does being focused help you find joy in life?

Practices to invite joyfulness

- Make a list of all the moments in your life that were really joyful.
- Do you see the world as evil or good? Is there hope or is life hopeless? If you see the world as evil, is there nothing in it that is good? Can you be happy in an evil world? Are you more likely to be happy in a good one?
- Take time to experience the ordinary.
- Lighten up and stop holding onto things so tightly.
- Invest in curiosity without judgment.
- Upset the patterns of your life in an uplifting way.
- Relax and let go of the need to control everything.
- Stop taking your life and spiritual practices so seriously.
- Look for the humor and joy in all things.
- Laugh.
- Hang out with little children – experience the world as they experience it.
- Look for the good.
- Be fresh.

Being Sacred

> *Not my will, but thine, be done.* (Matthew 22:42)

This is the essence and heart of the Christian teachings. When we completely let go of our ego and allow the Divine to guide us, that is when the Christos awakens within us. The secret is not to do what we want and dedicate it to GOD so as to justify bigotry, close mindedness, hatred, sexism, or ignorant attempts at saving the world. The secret is to live in a sacred manner, to recognize the sacredness of creation (1 Timothy 4:4), to walk according to the scriptures, to let go and allow the Divine to flow through us. In that state there is no nationality, no religion, race, gender, political affiliation, economic stature, or any other identifying characteristic: there is only GOD – for everything is Divine (Galatians 3:28 and Colossians 3:11).

It is hard to know much less believe that the Christos is within us. When we walk the Christian Path, giving ourselves completely over to it by embodying the teachings of Jesus: all doubt disappears. Just as when we first learn to play an instrument, we sound horrible. In time, as we continue to practice, we get better. Eventually our voice, our spirit begins to flow and express itself through the instrument. In the same way, when we begin to walk the Christian Path we are horrible. Our minds are filled with junk, we allow cravings, desires, and fears to chase and push us around, we are emotional wrecks, and so forth. When we do the practices, watch our minds, learn to let go, and live in a sacred manner, we become converted – we become holy:

> **But as he which hath called you is holy, so be ye holy in all you do; for it is written, Be ye holy; for I am Holy.** (1 Peter 15-16)

The first step towards this state is to become aware of our intentions, motivations, and desires. Are we doing it because we believe we know best or that the organization, religion, or order we belong to knows best? Are we acting for our own self-interests or for others? Do we intend to open the situation or merely use it? These and similar questions need to be asked as we begin treading this difficult Path.

The second step is to verbally, mentally, and physically dedicate everything we do to GOD: every time we sit down to eat, read, bathe, brush our teeth, pray, or whatever else we do, we dedicate it all to GOD: our actions, thoughts, and speech. Then we dedicate everything we do to others. If we are eating, we dedicate our food to those who have nothing to eat while wishing them health and abundance. Our prayers turn from selfish thankfulness and greedy pleas for help, to asking for the well-being of all – even those we hate. We no longer cling to the good things of our life, but instead send them out to those who are in need.

Compassion, love, thankfulness, humility, softness, and all the other Christ qualities begin to take root – they begin to flower in our lives. This is sacred – this is holy. It really makes a difference in life when we acknowledge everything that crosses our Path as sacred. Every person, every animal, every plant and particle – all this is GOD's creation: Is that not Sacred?

Things to contemplate

"But as he which hath called you is holy, so be ye holy in all you do; for it is written, Be ye holy; for I am Holy." (1 Peter 15-16)
- What is this verse saying?
- What is Holy?
- Can humans really be Holy?
- What are some signs of holiness?

"Not my will, but thine, be done." (Matthew 22:42)
- What does this verse mean to you?
- Define will.
- What things do you will for in life?
- Why would your will be different than GOD'S?

Practices to help invite sacredness

- Make a list of all your desires – how many of them are spiritual?
- This week write down every major choice you make. What were the motivations behind them?
- Verbally, physically, and mentally dedicate everything you do to GOD. Start with simple things like brushing your teeth, eating, drinking, taking a shower, etc. This practice does two things:
    1. Makes you completely aware of what you are doing.
    2. Gives your will and everything you do to GOD, which in turn, lessens the choke-hold the ego has on your consciousness.
- Read, study, and embody the scriptural teachings daily.
- Recognize that knowing the scriptures and living them are completely different. Knowing what we should do and doing it are different also!
- See the Spirit flowing through all things.
- Recognize how beautiful, precious, and meaningful life really is.
- Know that GOD is with us at all times.

Chapter Four
Growing from Practice

- Knowledge
- Virtue
- Giving/charity
- Patience
- Perseverance
- Temperance
- Humbleness
- Kindness
- Tranquility
- Wisdom

So far in this text we have prepared the field, planted the seeds, and rooted our minds. Now it is time to grow our branches. In this chapter there are ten essential practices the aspiring Christian embodies as they walk the Path. These ten practices are knowledge, virtue, charity, patience, perseverance, temperance, humbleness, kindness, tranquility, and wisdom.

With knowledge we learn about the Path and what it entails. Through virtue we become pure. With giving and charity we let go of the ego and embody the selfless nature of Christ. Having patience we till the soil of our lives so these seeds of Christ can grow. Strength through perseverance enables the roots to sink deep within us. Temperance helps us keep balanced. In being humble we let go and allow the Spirit to move through us. In kindness we give of ourselves unconditionally. With tranquility we find peace in all things, and in wisdom we share the fruits that have been given to us.

The first five practices find their completion in the last five. With knowledge comes wisdom. From virtuous action grows tranquility. By giving we invite kindness. Having patience we find humility, and with perseverance arises temperance.

Knowledge

> *By the law is the knowledge of sin.* (Romans 3:20)

This law is not a city ordinance that tells us what we can or cannot do. This verse points to the law of Truth which resides in all of us. It is our consciousness that knows what is healthy and what is harmful. Many of us have silenced this voice because we are so caught up in the reality we identify with. When we remember this knowledge and listen, that is when we have truly begun walking the Path.

> *We pray for you, and to desire that ye might be filled with the knowledge of his will in all wisdom and spiritual understanding; that ye might walk worthy of the Lord unto all pleasing, being fruitful in every good work, and increasing in the knowledge of* ***GOD****.* (Colossians 1:9-10)

Who would act unrighteously if they truly believed that every action, thought, and word that comes from them would always come back to them? What kind of person would waste their life when they understood how precious life is and how little time we have? How hard is it for us to go against our habits and beliefs? As we gain knowledge on the Path our will to go against the wholeness of these teachings lessens. In its place arises a yearning to awaken the Christos:

> *To know the love of Christ, which passeth knowledge, that ye might be filled with all the fullness of* ***GOD****.* (Ephesians 3:19)

Knowledge turns into wisdom through humility, learning, patience, practice, perseverance, experience, and integration. When we pray, contemplate, and practice these teachings with all our heart, mind, and soul – the Christos has begun to awaken within us.

Things to contemplate

"By the law is the knowledge of sin." (Romans 3:20)
- What is knowledge?
- What does it mean "by the law?"
- Research sin and write five different viewpoints of what it means. Do not be afraid to look at other philosophical and religious traditions besides Christianity.

"We pray for you, and to desire that ye might be filled with the knowledge of his will in all wisdom and spiritual understanding; that ye might walk worthy of the Lord unto all pleasing, being fruitful in every good work, and increasing in the knowledge of GOD." (Colossians 1:9-10)
- Put in your own words what this verse is saying.
- What does it mean "walk worthy of the Lord?"
- How can you increase your "knowledge of GOD?"
- What is the "knowledge of GOD?"

"To know the love of Christ, which passeth knowledge, that ye might be filled with all the fullness of GOD." (Ephesians 3:19)
- What is the "love of Christ?"
- What does "passeth knowledge" mean?
- What is it to know?
- How does knowing the love of Christ fill you with the "fullness of GOD?"

Practices to help invite knowledge

- Attend bible studies or start study groups.
- Read and meditate daily on the words of Jesus.
- Find as many different viewpoints as possible.
- Surround yourself with people who exemplify the teachings.
- Pray and meditate daily.
- Allow the sayings of Jesus to come into your daily activities.
- Recognize that there is no randomness and that every person, conversation, and thing you see and experience is the Spirit communicating to you in order to learn, become aware, and grow in Spirit.

Virtue

> *"What good thing shall I do, that I many have eternal life?" Jesus answered him, "Keep the Commandments."* (Matthew 19:16-21)

The second step on the Path is to refrain from unwholesome actions. This accomplishes two things: we no longer create negative karma and we free our minds from guilt, stress, and other unwanted emotions and thoughts. This is possible because we are acting in accordance with our conscience, and in doing so, we invite peace and clarity. While this is good, Jesus instructs us to go further. He tells us to turn the other cheek, avoid looking upon others lustfully, give to those in need, and to pray for those who attack us.

This is the ultimate good. When all our actions, thoughts, and words abide in this goodness, the seeds of Christ have begun to bare their fruits in our lives. It is not complicated, but it is not easy either. There is no one in the world who can claim to have become virtuous over night and there is no magic pill that will get us there either. It takes patience, acceptance, energy, effort, will, and love to find it. It helps to always be mindful of our actions, words, and thoughts, while at the same time having the intention to be virtuous. Eventually virtue awakens within us, and this virtue becomes an energy that can heal, calm, and enlighten others (Mark 5:30).

Things to contemplate

"What good thing shall I do, that I many have eternal life?" Jesus answered him, "Keep the commandments." (Matthew 19:16-21)
- What does Jesus say about the Commandments?
- What are the Commandments? Write about what each one means to you. Why are they important? Do you need to know the Commandments to know what is right and wrong?
- What is eternal life?

- Why does it say, "What good things shall I do" rather than "How shall I be?" Is there a difference?

Practices to help invite virtuous action

- Contemplate continuously on cause and effect.
- Be aware of all your actions, thoughts, and words and consider what they ultimately manifest in your life. Write down the results of each major action you do this week.
- Consciously choose your intention rather than go on autopilot. Write down those areas in your life that you allow autopilot to control you.
- Investigate your intentions: why do you act this way, do this thing, want this or that, et cetera...
- Contemplate on the Commandments and think about how they apply in the different areas of your life. For instance, socially, at work, at home, with family, and so forth.
- Meditate on the Commandments and allow their different levels to awaken within you. What subtleties are hidden within the Commandments? Is there more to them than meets the eye?

Giving/charity

> *And though I have the first of prophecy and understanding all mysteries and knowledge and thought and have all faith so that I could remove mountains, and have not charity, I am nothing* (1 Corinthians 13)

Without giving there is no life. GOD gave us breath and the earth gave us flesh – without giving we would not exist. One of the core teachings Jesus gave to us was to give. Give food to the hungry, drink to the thirsty, health to those who need to be healed, and light to all those who live in darkness. We are told in Matthew 5:15 that if we have a light we should not hide it under a bushel, but shine it for all to see by.

There are two types of giving: external and internal.

Some examples of external giving:
- Money
- Food
- Drink
- Clothing
- Shelter and warmth
- Transportation
- Bedding and other basic necessities
- Incense, oil, and perfume
- Sacred objects
- The Bible and other holy writings
- Lamps/light
- Tools

These twelve external objects represent a few things we can give to others. When we give it should be done with love and the desire to help. The process of giving is to fill a need and to lessen suffering so that our minds can be cleared in order to see the root of suffering and sever it. When we see something that is in need we offer our help without needing to be asked and we offer what is needed so that it is sufficient (Matthew 7:9). Giving is not about getting rid of our junk – giving is about letting go and opening the heart: that is the true practice of giving. It is a form of sacrifice that helps us break down the attachments that arise from greed and selfishness. When we give we are not trying to create more suffering or delusion such as when a weapon, poison, alcohol or some other mind altering substance or distraction is offered, nor do we give to feed another person's desires and attachments. We give what is needed and what will promote wholesomeness and abundance.

> *Do not sound a trumpet before thee, as the hypocrites do in the synagogues and the streets, that they may have glory of man. But when thy do they alms, let not thy left hand know what thy right hand doeth.* (Matthew 6:2)

We are to give in such a way that the receiver neither feels obligation nor embarrassment. As for those around who witness the practice, giving should not be done in such a manner that we are placed on a pedestal. We are not giving in the hope of some reward or honor. We give for Giving's sake, we give out of compassion, and we give to help end suffering. What we find when we give is that there is no difference between the giver and the receiver.

Examples of internal giving:
- Thoughts of compassion
- Dedications
- Mental thinking and visualizations
- Motivations
- Empowerment
- Letting go
- Non-attachment
- Selflessness
- Sacrificing desires, fears, anger, attachments, etc…
- Renunciation
- Prayer/Meditations

These twelve acts and others like unto them are a few things that we can give internally. These internal offerings often precede the external ones. It is the internal effort to overcome attachments that empower us to give externally. In many ways the internal giving not only precedes an external act, but follows them as well. For this reason an internal act of giving is far more beneficial to us and others.

We can give for many reasons: it can be unwholesome and harmful or beneficial and uplifting. We can give a lot or just a little. Whatever reason or amount, our motivations behind why we give will greatly affect us and the recipient:

> *And he looked up, and saw the rich men casting their gifts into the treasure. And he saw also a certain poor widow casting in thither two mites. And he said, of truth I say unto you, that this poor widow*

> *hath cast in more than they all: for all these have their abundance cast in unto the offering of GOD: but she of her penury hath cast in all the living that she had. (Luke 21:2-4)*

There are many motivations for giving. Some are genuinely healthy, while others are unwholesome. Below is a list of some motivations for giving:

- Reward
- Pressure
- Reputation
- Expectation
- Fear
- Favoritism
- Ill-will
- Shame and Guilt
- Delusion
- Sympathy
- Compassion
- Filling in a need or role
- Giving because it is good to give
- To help break the bonds of the ego and attachments
- Giving because it is inherently in our nature to give

So far we have seen that without giving we would not exist, that giving is the reason there is a Path, and without giving of ourselves we would not be on the Path. We have learned to practice charity in every situation and to everyone. We have spoken of external and internal giving and how we should go about practicing. We have seen some of the motivations that lead us into giving and learned that some are wholesome while others are unwholesome. Now we are going to speak about the five factors of giving and how the process of giving helps us on the Path.

There are five major factors of giving: the intention, the way that we give, the recipient, the gift, and the belief we hold about giving. As discussed above, the intention has a great influence on the effect/affect our giving will have on ourselves and others. The intention is like a planted seed; if the seed is rotten then the fruit of the tree will not bear forth.

The way we give greatly influences us and the receiver. Having love and a genuine sense of goodwill creates a bond of friendship and feelings of trust that will help both the giver and receiver grow and be fulfilled. It is good to avoid creating feelings of embarrassment, debt, or any thought that can lead to suffering. It is a gift to have opportunities to give and help – it is sacred. When we give it is to be done at the right time and at the right moment. If we were to give at the wrong moment there could result feelings of embarrassment and awkwardness. We are to give what is needed so as to sever any feelings of anxiety or fear of need. This is the basic idea of how we are to give.

The receiver is to be in need of something and the gift is to be something that fills their need. We should always be aware that some people will want things that they do not need or that they can acquire on their own. We are not obligated or bound to fulfill other people's desires or support their laziness. Giving is not some crutch that can be used against us when people feel like it. Giving is rooted in the essence of Christ; it is the Spirit that flows through us when there is a genuine need for something.

The gift is to be something which is usable and effective. We are not to give useless garbage. Why would anyone want our crap? The gift should be something wholesome like those things talked about in the external and internal giving earlier. We are not to give things that could cause harm or create more suffering for the receiver. The only time it is good to offer a poison, a drug, or something that otherwise would be harmful is when we give venom to counteract a snake bite, a drug to lessen pain, or a knife for surgery. The gift is something that helps end suffering not creates it. There is an old saying that helps us see the benefit of giving the right type of gift: "Feed a fish to a man and he will not hunger for the day, teach him how to fish and he will hunger no longer." A true gift is something that continues to unwrap itself. It strengthens and empowers both the giver and the receiver.

The view is the last major factor in giving. When giving we are to keep a clear understanding that according to the law of cause and effect, the generous act will bring beneficial results in the future. We are to contemplate that there is no "I" or "them", no internal or external giving, and that while giving we are to be aware that the gift, recipient, and giver are all connected together in the body of Christ. Our aim in giving is to always enhance ours and the recipient's efforts towards this realization (1 Corinthians 12:27). A second aspect of the correct view is to clear away all judgments, pity, disgust, guilt, duty, obligation, or any other belittling thought that leaves us feeling dirty or paints the receiver as being dirty.

Before we get into what we can do to help awaken charity within us there is a need to talk about what many Christians argue is really meant by giving. It is often argued that giving and charity is about giving the teachings of Jesus to others, rather than giving food, money, clothes, or whatnot. While the teachings are one of things we are to give, Jesus was emphatic when he said that he knew them not because they did not give him food when he was hungry and drink when thirsty (Matthew 25:35-45).

Too many Christians argue for or against certain teachings or completely ignore some verses as if they have no value in their life or contradict what they believe or wish to do. To be a Christian we cannot just pick and choose what things we want to follow. Being a Christian is about following in the footsteps of Jesus. That means doing what Jesus told us to do. Every word is important – to overlook anything is a mistake.

Things to contemplate

"And though I have the first of prophecy and understanding all mysteries and knowledge and thought and have all faith so that I could remove mountains, and have not charity, I am nothing" (1 Corinthians 13)

- What is this verse saying?
- Why would faith not be enough?
- Can you have faith and not do works?
- Define charity.

"Do not sound a trumpet before thee, as the hypocrites do in the synagogues and the streets, that they may have glory of man. But when thy do they alms, let not thy left hand know what thy right hand doeth." (Matthew 6:2)
- What does it mean not to let the left hand know what the right hand is doing?
- Why is it important to avoid giving in this way?
- Is giving money to the church or donating money to a charity all you need to do? Explain.

"And he looked up, and saw the rich men casting their gifts into the treasure. And he saw also a certain poor widow casting in thither two mites. And he said, of truth I say unto you, that this poor widow hath cast in more than they all: for all these have their abundance cast in unto the offering of GOD: but she of her penury hath cast in all the living that she had." (Luke 21:2-4)
- How did the poor lady give more than everyone else?
- What do you think about this verse?
- What relation does giving and sacrifice have?

Practices to help invite charity

- Give to a loved one randomly something that is dear to you
- Always take an opportunity to give to a street person when they are before you – even if that only means giving a dime or a nickel.
- Listen to what people need – it is amazing how many giving opportunities are missed. Even if giving is just to listen to someone's aches and pains, or to offer ideas, or give some spiritual support.
- When something happens to you that you would otherwise get angry over or in some way retaliate, take the moment to simply give away the situations instead of holding onto it.
- The very best time to give is when you find yourself holding onto something.
- Give yourself love!

Patience

> *On the good ground are they, which in an honest and good heart, having heard the word, keep it, and bring forth fruit with patience.* (Luke 8:15)

Some different areas in our lives that create opportunities for patience:

- Personal effort
- Time
- Tribulations
- Interactions
- Strangers
- Children
- Animals
- Communicating
- Driving
- Technology
- Goals
- Education
- Personal abilities or lack of
- Family
- Making money
- Waiting in line or for a light
- Relationships
- Entertainment
- Employment

There is an old story of a saint in the mountains who spent most of his life praying for patience. One day as he was praying in his hut a crazy old beggar came by. Being a great and compassionate person the saint invited the beggar into his hut and offered him what little food he had. The beggar went directly to the saints sleeping space and started knocking everything over to make himself comfortable. Sitting down, the miscreant rummaged through the saint's belongings, ripped pages from his Bible, spit on his cross, and all the while laughed obnoxiously at the pitiful state the saint was in. In pure amazement, the saint stared at this person with utter disbelief: 'Why would he do this to me,' he thought. The more the bum threw around his stuff and made fun of him, the more annoyed the saint became: 'Was it GOD testing him or maybe even the devil' he thought as irritation started to overcome him. At last, right as the dirty bum whispered into his ear that he was a fraud and all his prayers were nothing more than empty bags of gas, the saint exploded in rage and began to push this bothersome annoyance out of his hut. At the very moment the saint touched the beggar, a veil was lifted from his eyes enabling him to see the angel that was hidden behind the dirty clothes. With awe and reverence, he bowed to the glory of GOD; he learned at that moment that without others he could never truly embody patience. As the story goes, the saint came down from his mountain and was able to guide many people from darkness to the light because of his infinite patience.

> *Now we exhort you, brethren, warn them that are unruly, comfort the feebleminded, support the weak, be patient toward all men.* (1 Thessalonians 5:14)

    The most direct way to learn patience is to just do it by consciously bringing the mind to a state of acceptance and peace. It is hard to do this because we want things to be a certain way or to happen right now. The first step in learning patience is to open our eyes and learn to see the bigger picture. If someone has cut us off on the highway, maybe they received a call on their cell phone that their children are in the hospital. If it is our children who will not listen to us, maybe we need to stop and listen to them first. The point of seeing the bigger picture is to give us a different and wider perspective of the situation. The more we can see and understand, the more accepting we become.
    What we learn in life is that patience comes only through experience. We can have all the patience in the world until that situation comes up that makes patience go out the window.

The idea behind this is to teach us not to run from life and expect that one day we will learn how to be more patient and compassionate. What we need to do – is to do it! There is no other way. It is through our interactions, attachments, and desires that we are given the opportunity to learn how to be patient. When we can consciously bring our mind towards this practice – patience naturally follows. Without it, the Path of Christ will not bear forth its fruits.

Things to contemplate

"Now we exhort you, brethren, warn them that are unruly, comfort the feebleminded, support the weak, be patient toward all men." (1 Thessalonians 5:14)
- What is patience?
- Why should you be patient with everyone and everything?
- How can procrastination, fear, and avoidance be mistaken for patience?
- Can patience be a bad thing? If so, when?

"On the good ground are they, which in an honest and good heart, having heard the word, keep it, and bring forth fruit with patience." (Luke 8:15)
- What is this verse saying?
- What are the key words?
- Why is patience needed to bring forth fruit?

Practices to help invite patience
- Make a list of all the things that test your patience.
- Try to see the bigger picture.
- Avoid feeding impatient thoughts.
- Let go by opening yourself to the situation instead of being driven by it.
- Focus on the emotion rather than the story line/situation.
- Breathe.
- Consciously take the moment to enhance your ability to be patient by recognizing that here is an opportunity to be patient and so you take it. This is a great technique when you are driving on a curvy road behind a slow driver who refuses to pull over☺

Perseverance

> *Ye shall be hated of all men for my name's sake: but he that endureth to the end shall be saved.* (Matthew 11:22)

Patience without perseverance is hopeless and shallow. Like the seed which is sown upon the stony ground, without perseverance we cannot grow the roots we need to bring nourishment and abundance into our lives.

> *These are they likewise which are sown on stony ground; who, when they have heard the word, immediately receive it with gladness; and have no root in themselves, and so endure but for a time: afterward, when affliction or persecution ariseth for the word's sake, immediately they are offended.* (Mark 4:16-17)

Perseverance helps us overcome laziness. It supports us when inspiration has gone away and it strengthens us when we are weak and doubtful. The following four forms of laziness hinder our efforts to walk the Path:

- *Listless and tired:* Sleep overwhelms us. Every time we find a moment to pray, study, or meditate, we are too tired and too drained to focus.
- *Idleness:* Sitting around watching TV, listening to the radio, reading entertaining stories, etc...
- *Disregard:* Falling into doubt, not trusting in ourselves or in the Sprit and so we regard the effort it takes to walk the Path as being worthless and a waste of time.
- *Gross:* Spending extra effort creating opportunities to distract ourselves.

Three tools of perseverance are focus, concentration, and awareness. When we have these three things we are able to avoid and overcome the traps of laziness.

The two major benefits of perseverance are:

- Ability to attain our desired aims
- Ability to accumulate virtue by being:
    1. *Unshakable:* To persevere through any opposition, doubt, or affliction
    2. *Joyful:* To persevere with joy and happiness
    3. *Humble:* To persevere without getting caught up in pride or egotism

When we first start walking the Path all these practices are new and exciting and so are easy to work with. This feeling does not last. Once the fun has gone and the real work begins, that is when we come to understand perseverance. In time we learn how difficult it is to be a Christian and how hard it is to carry our *own* cross. Endurance helps us overcome our weaknesses and it gives us the strength to let go and overcome tribulations, doubt, and all the other challenges that arise on our Path. To find this endurance we must have a strong will and a willingness to walk the Path.

Things to contemplate

"Ye shall be hated of all men for my name's sake: but he that endureth to the end shall be saved." (Matthew 11:22)
- What is this verse saying?
- Define perseverance?
- Does endurance give room to procrastination, dereliction, forgetfulness, etc?
- Why is endurance necessary?
- Give one example of something in your life that would not have come to fruition without persevering.

"These are they likewise which are sown on stony ground; who, when they have heard the word, immediately receive it with gladness; and have no root in themselves, and so endure but for a time: afterward, when affliction or persecution ariseth for the word's sake, immediately they are offended." (Mark 4:16-17)
- What is this verse saying?
- How have you seen this in your life?

Practice to help invite perseverance

- Meditate on the three virtuous qualities of perseverance: unshakable, joyful, and humble.
- Constantly remember impermanence.
- Think about the benefits of these teachings.
- Think of every possible excuse not to do these or similar practices.
- Focus on what you are doing all the time. Work on overcoming the autopilot mode.
- When a distraction comes up, bring you mind to it instead of simply allowing it to overcome you. Analyze it. Ask yourself why you want to do it. Imagine this moment as your last on earth and ask yourself what you want to be doing right now.
- What do you really want? Do you want to embody these qualities? Really? Be truthful. If this is what you really want, than perseverance will not be a problem.

Temperance

Let your moderation be known unto all men. (Philippians 4:5)

There are three things to consider when we look at temperance. The first is restraint – to withhold ourselves from those actions that lead to temptation. We know what leads us away from the Path. If it is sexual desire, then we know what images, movies, thoughts, and people will trigger our temptation. If we are easily distracted, then we should be focused and have a plan to undertake when distractions arise. The idea behind restraint is to be preemptive, to know what triggers our issues and to create a plan that will minimize if not eliminate them.

The second thing to consider is self-control. This is necessary when we are unable to avoid those situations that cause us trouble. Instead of avoiding certain actions and situations we learn to control our minds by refusing to feed those thoughts that ignite and inflame temptation.

> *Watch and pray, that ye enter not into temptation: the spirit indeed is willing, but the flesh is weak.*
> (Matthew 26:41)

The last aspect of temperance to consider is balance and harmony. We avoid becoming drill sergeants who force every moment to be a certain way and we avoid becoming a slacker who avoids taking initiative: not too tight and not too loose. We are not trying to starve ourselves into martyrdom nor punish ourselves because we are sinful. Neither are we to use Christian theology as a means to justify our actions in the world or to use our beliefs as a means to place ourselves above others as if to imply our truth is the only truth. When we are balanced, the Spirit moves through us. That is when we find harmony in our lives. We do not need to premeditate or worry, for the Spirit is with us at all times.

As temperance takes hold we begin to notice the extremes leveling out. What replaces these extreme ups and downs is peace, balance, and serenity.

Things to contemplate

"Let your moderation be known unto all men." (Philippians 4:5)
- Define moderation.
- Are you moderate? If so, in what areas of your life?
- How can you let your moderation be known to all without giving rise to egotism?
- What is tempering?

"Watch and pray, that ye enter not into temptation: the spirit indeed is willing, but the flesh is weak." (Matthew 26:41)
- What are you to watch? Television?
- What does it mean to "watch?"
- How does prayer help overcome temptation?
- What is the flesh?
- What does it mean, "the spirit is willing?"

Practice to help invite temperance

- Make a list of your triggers.
- Make a list of what actions to take when you find yourself in situations that challenge you.
- Memorize the sayings of Jesus and use them for support when temptation arises.
- Do not be so hard on yourself – Do not be too soft either!

Humbleness

> *Whosoever will be great among you, let him be your minister; and whosoever will be chief among you, let him be your servant.* (Matthew 20:26-27)

Humbleness embraces, softens, steps back, slows down, and opens us to the Christos. It is a word that defines gentleness and understanding while inviting love and compassion. Humbleness is also a rock, harder than the densest stone – it is the cornerstone that holds the teachings of Jesus together. In its simplest state it leaves no one behind, nor does it invite fear, aggression, competition, or closed-mindedness. Humbleness is the great embodiment of Christ – for we are here to serve – not to rule.

The humble are like the backstage worker whose efforts enable the show to unfold. They do not brag of their kindness, show off how charitable they are, or flaunt how much they suffer in their fasting and sacrifice. Humility is like a soft cushion for all to rest on. It allows the Divine to work through us without judgment, desire, attachment, regret, or fear getting in the way.

> *I thank thee, O Father, Lord of heaven and earth, because thou hast hid these things from the wise and prudent and hast revealed them unto babes.* (Matthew 11:25)

Humbleness does have a downside. It can become another game we play with ourselves. Humbleness can become a competition and it can become another source of pride. Humility has a strange way of uplifting and placing us upon a pedestal. We can look so good before others that they will give to us out of respect. We can be so honored in our ascetic fasts and practices that those who see us will hold feasts in our name. We can pray so loudly and eloquently that those who hear us will bask in our glory and seek to inflate us further with their prayers. By uplifting ourselves we are brought down in the sight of the Lord:

> *For every one that exalteth himself shall be abased, and he that humbleth himself shall be exalted.* (Luke 18:14)

This is not saying we should debase ourselves and become mediocre with the things that we are good at. We should always do the best that we can while constantly challenging ourselves to improve. It is the competitiveness and struggle that comes with being the best over others that creates separation and conceit. It is that kind of thinking that blocks us from being open and humble. How can compassion arise when we harbor such self-cherishing thoughts? To have compassion for others is to lift them above ourselves. The following verses share some practices we can do to help invite humbleness in our lives:

> *Take heed that ye do not your alms before men, to be seen of others: otherwise ye have no reward of your Father which is in Heaven. Therefore, when thou doest thine alms, do not sound a trumpet before thee, as the hypocrites do in the synagogues and in the streets, that they may have glory of men. Verily I say unto you, they have their reward. But when thou doest alms, let not thy left hand know what thy right hand doeth; that thine alms may be in secret; and thy Father which seeth in secret himself shall reward thee openly.* (Matthew 6:1-4)

Charity is not something we do to gain reward, be acknowledged, manipulate our taxes, or create bitterness, dependency, and feelings of worthlessness in others. When we give it is to be done with love, selflessness, and non-judging. It is a practice we work on, not an act that we do. We are learning to let go of desire, selfishness, and egotism so that we can awaken the Christos within ourselves. This is possible when we have truly let go of our self-centeredness (Matthew 10:39). The next practice deals with prayer.

> *When thou prayest, thou shalt not be as the hypocrites are; for they love to pray standing in the synagogues and in the corners of the streets, that they may be seen of men. Verily I say unto you, they have their reward. But thou, when thou prayest, enter into thy closet and when thou hast shut thy door, pray to thy Father which is in secret; and thy Father which seeth in secret shall reward thee openly. But when ye pray, use not vain repetitions, as the heathens do: for they think that they shall be heard for their much speaking. Be not ye therefore like unto them: for your Father knoweth what things ye have need of, before ye ask him.* (Matthew 6:5-8)

Our prayers are not to be seen or heard by others but spoken from within our heart. When we pray externally our attention, energy, and design is focused on the world. When we pray internally our attention, energy, and focus is directed towards the Divine that resides within us. True prayer is not some incantation or invocation of the magician so as to persuade and force the spirits to do our will. Nor is it a shopping list to GOD to bring us wealth, fame, or any other selfish aim. Prayer opens us to the Divine, giving us an opportunity to let go of ourselves in order to reveal the Christos within. A next practice deals with fasting and all the different practices we undertake.

> *When ye fast, be not, as the hypocrites, of a sad countenance; for they disfigure their faces, that they*

> *may appear unto men to fast. Verily I say unto you, they have their reward. But thou, when thou fastest, anoint thine head, and wash thy face; that thou appear not unto men to fast, but unto the Father, which seeth in secret, shall reward thee openly.*
> (Matthew 6:16-19)

Martyrism is not the key to Christianity. Nor is it about flaunting our strength or showing how much weight we put on our shoulders. Being a Christian is not about letting others know how humble we are, how much we give, how often we pray, how long we fast, how frequently we go to church, or how much we suffer. We anoint ourselves and wash our face of all pride so as to be a pure reflection of others potential rather than a mirror of their weaknesses. The real work happens underneath the surface. As we grow the light of our practices will break through the surface as a flower from the seeds of the earth. It just takes time and a lot of effort, patience, compassion, and understanding. Being humble is one of the greatest tools we have towards awakening the Christos.

Things to contemplate

"Whosoever will be great among you, let him be your minister; and whosoever will be chief among you, let him be your servant." (Matthew 20:26-27)
- How could this work in reality?
- How is this different from what you are taught in the world?
- Define humbleness.
- How does humility come up in your life?

"For every one that exalteth himself shall be abased, and he that humbleth himself shall be exalted." (Luke 18:14)
- How do you exalt yourself?
- What things do you want to be acknowledged for?
- How do you feel when being acknowledge?

"Take heed that ye do not your alms before men, to be seen of others: otherwise ye have no reward of your Father which is in Heaven. Therefore, when thou doest thine alms, do not sound a trumpet before thee, as the hypocrites do in the synagogues and in the streets, that

they may have glory of men. Verily I say unto you, they have their reward. But when thou doest alms, let not thy left hand know what thy right hand doeth; that thine alms may be in secret; and thy Father which seeth in secret himself shall reward thee openly." (Matthew 6:1-4)

- Having worked with giving earlier in the text, what could be the next level of giving?
- How can you give yourself to GOD?

"When thou prayest, thou shalt not be as the hypocrites are; for they love to pray standing in the synagogues and in the corners of the streets, that they may be seen of men. Verily I say unto you, they have their reward. But thou, when thou prayest, enter into thy closet and when thou hast shut thy door, pray to thy Father which is in secret; and thy Father which seeth in secret shall reward thee openly. But when ye pray, use not vain repetitions, as the heathens do: for they think that they shall be heard for their much speaking. Be not ye therefore like unto them: for your Father knoweth what things ye have need of, before ye ask him." (Matthew 6:5-8)

- How often do you pray?
- What do you use prayer for?
- What do you pray for?
- When, where, and how do you pray?

"When ye fast, be not, as the hypocrites, of a sad countenance; for they disfigure their faces, that they may appear unto men to fast. Verily I say unto you, they have their reward. But thou, when thou fastest, anoint thine head, and wash thy face; that thou appear not unto men to fast, but unto the Father, which seeth in secret, shall reward thee openly." (Matthew 6:16-19)

- Do you fast?
- What is the purpose of fasting?
- How many people do you know fast?
- When you take a burden on your shoulders how do you act? Do you make a point of letting others know? Do you grumble?

Practices to help invite humility

- Hide the good things you do from others.
- Instead of talking – listen!
- Pray a lot.
- Offer up good things to others instead of taking them for yourself.
- When the last of something comes – do not take it.
- When the chance to take the lesser portion arises – take it.

- Open the door for others.
- Respect other people's beliefs and philosophies.
- Trust in GOD and let go.
- Allow other people the glory of the things you do.
- Meditate on being a speck of sand in GOD'S creation.
- Know that death comes to all.
- Be honest with others and be honest with yourself. It is okay to be screwed up. When you are able to be honest with yourself, that is when you can truly change and begin to have control over your life.

Kindness

> ***Be ye kind one to another.*** *(Ephesians 4:32)*

There are many words we can use to help us understand what kindness is:

- Giving
- Understanding
- Thoughtfulness
- Consideration
- Gentleness
- Respectful
- Benevolence
- Helpful
- Forgiving
- Loving
- Empathy
- Compassion
- Etc…

All these words convey different aspects of kindness. Kindness is a sublime state of giving because it gives a part of ourselves to others. It should not be confused with compromising, giving in, or being weak. Kindness never leaves a feeling of obligation, doubt, or animosity. It opens the heart of all those who witness its presence.

Though I speak with the tongues of men and of angels, and have not charity, I am become as sounding brass, or a tinkling cymbal. And though I have the gift of prophecy, and understand all mysteries, and all knowledge; and though I have all faith, so that I could remove mountains, and have not charity, I am nothing. And though I bestow all my goods to feed the poor, and though I give my body to be burned, and have not charity, it profiteth me nothing. Charity suffereth long, and is kind; charity envieth not; charity vaunteth not itself, is not puffed up, Doth not behave itself unseemly, seeketh not her own, is not easily provoked, thinketh no evil; Rejoiceth not in iniquity, but rejoiceth in the truth; Beareth all things, believeth all things, hopeth all things, endureth all things. Charity never faileth: but whether there be prophecies, they shall fail; whether there be tongues, they shall cease; whether there be knowledge, it shall vanish away. For we know in part, and we prophesy in part. But when that which is perfect is come, then that which is in part shall be done away. When I was a child, I spake as a child, I understood as a child, I thought as a child: but when I became a man, I put away childish things. For now we see through a glass, darkly; but then face to face: now I know in part; but then shall I know even as also I am known. And now abideth faith, hope, charity, these three; but the greatest of these is charity. (1 Corinthians 13)

Things to contemplate

"Be ye kind one to another." (Ephesians 4:32)
- Define kindness.
- Make a list of all the people in your life that have shown you kindness.
- What is this verse saying?
- Make a list of all those times someone did not show you kindness. How did you feel?

"Though I speak with the tongues of men and of angels, and have not charity, I am become as sounding brass, or a tinkling cymbal. And though I have the gift of prophecy, and understand all mysteries, and all knowledge; and though I have all faith, so that I could remove mountains, and have not charity, I am nothing. And though I bestow all my goods to feed the poor, and though I give my body to be burned, and have not charity, it profiteth me nothing. Charity suffereth long, and is kind; charity envieth not; charity vaunteth not itself, is not puffed up, Doth not behave itself unseemly, seeketh not her own, is not easily provoked, thinketh no evil; Rejoiceth not in iniquity, but rejoiceth in the truth; Beareth all things, believeth all things, hopeth all things, endureth all things. Charity never faileth: but whether there be prophecies, they shall fail; whether there be tongues, they shall cease; whether there be knowledge, it shall vanish away. For we know in part, and we prophesy in part. But when that which is perfect is come, then that which is in part shall be done away. When I was a child, I spake as a child, I understood as a child, I thought as a child: but when I became a man, I put away childish things. For now we see through a glass, darkly; but then face to face: now I know in part; but then shall I know even as also I am known. And now abideth faith, hope, charity, these three; but the greatest of these is charity." (1 Corinthians 13)

- Why would faith not be enough?
- What is this verse saying?
- Why is giving to the poor and giving your body to the flames not necessarily charity?
- What is charity? What is the connection between giving and kindness?
- Make a list of those times you failed to show kindness. Why were you not kind?

Practices to help invite kindness

- Really listen. Not only to what others say but also to what you are thinking and feeling. When you pray: listen.
- Be helpful. Become the hand of GOD. Do and act as GOD would do. While not all can heal, there is comfort. If you cannot prophesize, maybe you can offer words of encouragement. Become the channel from which GOD can touch the world.
- Forgive. You are told to forgive not once, but as often as needs be (Matthew18:21). Forgiveness is at the core of salvation. Without forgiving others their trespasses, GOD will not forgive yours (Matthew 6:15).
- Make a list of everyone you have issues with. Write out how you feel and think about each of them, and then begin the process of forgiving them. It is not easy. At first your forgiveness might slide

from your lips with no real thought or feeling behind them, but continue past the words. Send them good thoughts, wish them well, pray for their health and happiness. When doing this you will begin to see just how hard it is to forgive. It is not lip service – it is a painful, difficult, and sometimes impossible task to undertake. Every time you find yourself thinking about this person or situation in your life, wish them well; especially when you find yourself thinking harmful and hurtful thoughts towards them. This is the key moment of forgiveness.
- Whenever you hear a fire engine or ambulance, take the moment to breathe and send a blessing with them. Wish for those who suffer to be free from their suffering, those who are sick or in pain to be free from their pain, and those who are afraid and alone to be comforted.
- Be nice with your words, thoughts, and actions.

Tranquility/Peace

> *Peace I leave with you, my peace I give unto you: not as the world giveth, give I unto you. Let not your heart be troubled, neither let it be afraid.* (John 14:27)

Tranquility comes through effort, virtue, contentment, openness, trust, and love. Like the dancer who has lived their art until they have attained the seamless performance of simplicity and like the artist and musician who have attained perfection and transcendence through continual practice, so is tranquility born from virtuous actions, purified bodies, clarified minds, a harmonized will, and the realization and embodiment of unsurpassable faith (Conviction).

> *And he said unto them, 'Why are ye fearful, o ye of little faith?' then he arose, and rebuked the winds and the sea; and there was a great calm.* (Matthew 8:26)

Like the winds and sea, our minds are lost in the turmoil of fears, desires, doubts, passions, guilt, attachments, anger, and many other strong emotions and thoughts. When we gain control of our minds through faith and effort, we will find the calmness of the sea. When we can sink into ourselves and rest in the peace of perfect trust – our minds, thoughts, emotions, and desires calm down and become peaceful.

> *Let your moderation be known unto all men. The Lord is at hand. Be careful for nothing; but in everything by prayer and supplication with thanksgiving let your requests be made known unto GOD. And the peace of GOD, which passeth all understanding, shall keep your hearts and minds through Christ Jesus.* (Philippians 4:5-7)

By moderation, keeping a vigilant awareness of our thoughts, and walking in a Sacred manner, we open ourselves to receive the peace of GOD (Tranquility). Philippians continues on to talk about being true, honest, just, pure, loving, good, and virtuous as a means to attain the presence of the Lord of Peace. It is through these actions that we find peace, and with this peace, live tranquilly. Another action we can take towards inviting this peace is to be content with what is before us:

> *Not that I speak in respect of want; for I have learned, in whatsoever state I am, therewith to be content.* (Philippians 4:6)

Through contentment we no longer suffer the pains of jealousy and desire. When we are free from the fetters of desire, fear, hatred, and ignorance, we awaken peace in our lives.

Things to contemplate

"Peace I leave with you, my peace I give unto you: not as the world giveth, give I unto you. Let not your heart be troubled, neither let it be afraid." (John 14:27)
- Define tranquility.
- What is this verse saying?
- Make a list of all the things you are afraid of.
- Make a list of all the things that trouble you in your life.

"And he said unto them, 'Why are ye fearful, o ye of little faith?' then he arose, and rebuked the winds and the sea; and there was a great calm." (Matthew 8:26)

- What does fear have to do with having little faith?
- How does emotional and mental turmoil affect your faith?
- What is the connection between having faith and finding peace?

"Let your moderation be known unto all men. The Lord is at hand. Be careful for nothing; but in everything by prayer and supplication with thanksgiving let your requests be made known unto GOD. And the peace of GOD, which passeth all understanding, shall keep your hearts and minds through Christ Jesus." (Philippians 4:5-7)

- What does moderation, being vigilant, praying, and being thankful have to do with peace?
- What does "be careful for nothing" mean?
- What is the "peace of GOD?"

Practices to help invite tranquility

- Meditate on GOD.
- Trust in GOD.
- Weaken attachments, desires, and fears by confronting them and then letting them go.
- Find contentment with what you have.
- Follow the Ten Commandments to perfection. This invites tranquility because there is nothing to fear from your actions. It is peaceful to know that at any moment the walls can drop down around you and there would be nothing to be ashamed about if anyone saw what you were doing, speaking, or thinking.
- Tranquility comes when you have complete faith – for there is truly nothing to fear.
- Be moderate in everything you do.
- Constantly be thankful for everything.
- Always have a heart filled with prayer.
- Remember you have control of your state of mind and emotional state.
- Be joyful and happy!
- Embrace the beauty of GOD's creation.
- Embrace simplicity.
- Enjoy the small things in life.
- Walk in a Sacred manner.
- See everything as Divine.

Wisdom

> But the WISDOM that is from above is first pure, then peaceable, gentle, and easy to be entreated, full of mercy and good fruits, without partiality, and without hypocrisy. *(James 3:17)*

Wisdom is not something we can buy nor learn. It is the fruit of practice – the pinnacle of embracing and walking the Path. The mind is not clouded by mental and emotional imbalances nor rippled by desires, fears and attachments of the world. All worldly affections have dissolved and what remains is a pure spring flowing forth from the heart. Wisdom is peace and unity – not dispersion and separation. Wisdom is gentle, moderate, and a reflection of the Divine. Wisdom arises when our practices have become a way of being. True wisdom does not care for praise or blame and it is impartial to class, color, gender, religion, philosophy, or any other characteristic which separates us from one another. There is no guile, no fear, and no doubt.

> **Be ye therefore perfect, even as your Father which is in heaven is perfect.** *(Matthew 5:48)*

> **Know ye not that your body is the temple of the Holy Ghost.** *(1 Corinthians 6:18-20)*

> **The Kingdom of GOD is within you.** *(Luke 17:21)*

Wisdom cannot be taught nor caught – it blossoms from within. The only practices i know of that can help unfold wisdom is meditation, prayer, recognizing the Omnipresence of Divinity, and walking a Sacred Path. One thing is for certain, when wisdom blossoms, all separation disappears.

> *That they all may be one; as thou, Father, art in me, and I in thee, that they also may be one in us: that the world may believe that thou hast sent me. And the glory which thou gavest me I have given them:*

that they may be one, even as we are one. I in them, and thou in me, that they may be made perfectly one. (John 17:21-23)

Things to contemplate

"But the WISDOM that is from above is first pure, then peaceable, gentle, and easy to be entreated, full of mercy and good fruits, without partiality, and without hypocrisy." (James 3:17)
- Define wisdom?
- What is worldly wisdom?
- What is spiritual wisdom?
- What are the good fruits of wisdom?

"Be ye therefore perfect, even as your Father which is in heaven is perfect." (Matthew 5:48)
- Is it possible to be perfect?
- What is perfection?
- Why would Jesus tell you to do something impossible?

"Know ye not that your body is the temple of the Holy Ghost" (1 Corinthians 6:18-20)
- What is the Holy Ghost?
- How could your body be considered a temple? Does this mean you should worship the body or worship from within the body?
- What is this verse saying?

"The Kingdom of GOD is within you." (Luke 17:21)
- What is the kingdom of GOD?
- What is this verse saying?
- How are you taught about this in church?
- What is the Kingdom of Heaven? Is that something different from the Kingdom of GOD?
- What does it mean the "Kingdom of Heaven is at hand?"

Practices to help invite wisdom

- Do the practices in this text.
- Meditate regularly.

- Contemplate the Sacred Scriptures and embody their wisdom.
- Be present.
- Become like a child.
- Embody the teachings of Jesus.
- Be free of judgment.
- Pray unceasingly.
- Let go of attachments.
- Stop believing that you know what is right and what is wrong.
- Answer this question daily: "Are you separate from the world or one with it?"
- Be truthful with yourself.
- See life as a lesson to be learned and then learn it.
- Look deeply into life.
- See the Sacredness of life.
- Recognize that GOD's creation is not evil – it is Sacred!

Chapter Five
Cultivating the Path

- Turning adversity into a practice
- Becoming like a child
- Faith

Cultivation helps weed out the unwanted things, nourishes, supports, and enriches the soil, strengthens the plants, and harmonizes the environment. The three practices in this chapter give us the when, how, and why. When do we practice? Whenever there is adversity, unbalance, friction, trouble, fear, desire, etc... How do we practice? As a child, as one who is open, receptive, attentive, joyful, simple, and so on. And why do we practice? Because we have faith that these practices help us awaken the Christos.

Turning adversity into a practice

> *That ye resist not evil: but whosoever shall smite thee on thy right cheek, turn to him the other also. And if any man will sue thee at the law, and take away thy coat, let him have thy cloak also. (Matthew 5:39-40)*

Here it is. In the Old Testament we take an eye for an eye, but as Gandhi is claimed to have said, "an eye for an eye will leave everyone blind." Jesus taught us to go beyond the Law – he taught us how to find perfection. And yet, many of us still ask: "Why should we love our enemy or bless those who curse us? What good does that do?"

> *For if you love them which love you, what reward have ye? Do not even the publicans the same? And if ye salute your brethren only, what do you have more than others? Do not even the publicans so? Be ye therefore perfect, even as your Father which is in heaven is perfect. (Matthew 5:46-48)*

Suffering is a big part of life – even for those with abundance. What we find as we walk our Path is that those things which bring the most change in our lives are often the very things we would never want to happen. It would be nice to have infinite patience while never having to use it. It's through practice and cultivation that the fruit is brought forth. If we never sharpen and oil our knives, they will be dull. And so, if we do not keep our minds and practices oiled and sharpened, we will not find patience, compassion, and understanding.

When we avoid the misery in life we often cause ourselves more suffering. Fighting against and running from the uncomfortable and unwanted situations, people, and things in our lives end up separating us from life itself, and in doing that, cause us greater pain. We spend more time running away from the uncomfortable situations in our lives and working towards securing our future that we fail to enjoy the fruits of life and the blessings of being alive right here, right now.

All the practices in this text help us slow down, be present, and embody the qualities of Christ within ourselves. It is not easy – to think otherwise is to be a fool. The last thing we want in life is to actually feel the pain, experience the suffering, and work through our junk. We want to be happy, we want to enjoy our lives, we want abundance, wealth, health, and joy. Why the heck would we ever wish to venture in this direction? Why would we ever want to carry our own cross – isn't Jesus carrying it for us? There is no easy answer. The truth is, most of us are not ready to walk with Jesus. I know this is hard to hear, but the teachings of Jesus were never meant for the masses, there were meant for the elite of the elite. For those who truly wish to walk with GOD – we must let go of this world and follow in the footsteps of Jesus. Does this mean we are all damned? No. It just means we have a long way to go. When we are ready to let go of our desires, attachments, fears, doubts, and most of all, our egos, Jesus is there to show us the way. Until then, follow the Commandments, work on letting go, and whenever the opportunity arises, practice. Practice! Practice!

> *My brethren, count it all joy when ye fall into divers temptations; Knowing this, that the trying of your faith worketh patience.* (James 1:2-3)

We should not delude ourselves into thinking that one day our suffering will disappear. Instead, we are to become more aware of the world's suffering, which in turn lessens the intensity of our own while inviting compassion into our lives.

Benefits of transforming suffering into a practice:
- Enables growth
- Opens us to life rather than closing us off from it
- Makes us stronger
- Gives us opportunities to help others
- Transforms us
- Invites peace into our lives
- Breaks the chains of fear, aversion, hatred, anger, and desire
- There is plenty of opportunity
- Empowers us to overcome adversity
- Turns suffering into a blessings
- Gives us true understanding

Some of the classic ways to deal with pain:
- *Rationalizing* until the emotion is gone
- *Anger* should be a four letter word
- *Depression* or is it suppression
- *Getting down* town on our selves
- *Denial* is not a river in Egypt
- *Humor* away the tears
- *Poor me* syndrome
- Apocalyptic *Martyrism*
- The *blame* game
- We get what we *deserve*
- Living in a *fantasy* world

Some examples of how Jesus instructs us to deal with adversity:
- Turning the other cheek (Matthew 5:39)
- Workers in the field (Matthew 20:1-13)
- Giving the cloak (Matthew 5:40)

- Coin to Caesar (Matthew 17:27)
- Beam in the eye (Matthew 7:3)
- Taking up our own cross (Matthew 10:38)
- Live by the sword, die by the sword (Matthew 26:52)
- Love thy enemy (Matthew 5:44)
- Agree with thy adversary (Matthew 5:25)

The story of Job is a good example of how we can turn adversity into a practice. Cars break down, our neighbor's dog poops everywhere and barks all the time, people get laid off, children get sick, things get lost, people die, ad infinitum. We always have a choice. We can either get caught up in the same old habitual patterns and responses or we can grow from the experience. One takes us down the same old road while the other takes us somewhere else. Sometimes it might feel worse and other times it might feel better. The point is that it is something new. It does not leave us with a heavy heart but with an open one, and it does not leave a sour taste in our lives but a fresh one. The difference between these two choices is that one moves us towards change while the other just further solidifies the same old unwanted behaviors and responses.

We cannot control life; the only things we can control are our emotional reactions and our thoughts. If we can understand this, then we have already taken the first step towards transforming our lives

Turning adversity into a practice is not condoning the action itself. We are not excusing the action; we are merely using it as a means towards growth. While it might appear to some that we are weak and neglectful fools who avoid the dramas of life, what we find in practice is strength, empowerment, and openness. Better it be that we are ridiculed and hated for the good actions we do, than be admired for hatred, anger, and whatever other emotion that arises when we are caught up.

Things to contemplate

"That ye resist not evil: but whosoever shall smite thee on thy right cheek, turn to him the other also. And if any man will sue thee at the law, and take away thy coat, let him have thy cloak also." (Matthew 5:39-40)
- What is this verse saying?
- How does this verse sit with society? Explain answer.
- How do you feel about this verse?
- Is this something you practice in life? Why or why not?

"For if you love them which love you, what reward have ye? Do not even the publicans the same? And if ye salute your brethren only, what do you have more than others? do not even the publicans so? Be ye therefore perfect, even as your Father which is in heaven is perfect." (Matthew 5:46-48)
- Why does Jesus make this point?
- What is Jesus pointing out?
- Can you be perfect as the Father who is in heaven is perfect? Explain answer.

"My brethren, count it all joy when ye fall into divers temptations; Knowing this, that the trying of your faith worketh patience." (James 1:2-3)
- Why should you be joyful for temptations?
- How does temptations invite patience?
- Do you agree? Explain answer.

Practices to help transform adversity into practice

- When you are bored – that is the moment to practice.
- When you are stressed, anxious, nervous, scared, desireful – that is the moment to practice.
- When you are happy, joyful, ecstatic – that is the moment to practice.
- When you notice yourself being out of balance – that is the moment to practice.
- When you are caught up – that is the moment to practice.
- When you are angry, jealous, frustrated, lustful, etc. – that is the moment for practice.
- When you are hitting every red light, when children are crying, when you do not care anymore – that is the moment to practice.

Become like a child

> *Verily I say unto you, except ye be converted, and become as little children, ye shall not enter unto the kingdom of heaven.* (Matthew 18:2)

Why is faith and works not enough to get into Heaven? Why must we also become like little children? Below is a list of some spiritual qualities little children naturally exhibit:

- No separation between self and others
- Quick to let things go
- Open to life
- Uninhibited in thought
- Telling the truth with no regard of consequence
- As babes they have no hidden aspects
- Experience life as it is
- Direct and to the point insights
- Not overly serious
- Willing to play
- Unconditional love
- Needing guidance, support, and protection
- Innocent
- No malice
- No guile
- Rarely envious
- Etc…

While this list is not complete it does give us an idea of what Jesus was pointing to. Of course, these qualities are not always present in children and when they are present they are not necessarily originating from an enlightened mind. Even so, by witnessing these qualities in action we can reflect on them and strive to embody them in our lives.

> *Wherefore laying aside all malice, and all guile, and hypocrisies, and envies, and evil speaking. As newborns babes, desire the sincere milk of the word, that ye may grow thereby.* (1 Peter 2:1)

If we look at all the different quotes dealing with this topic we hear Jesus telling us to become *as* or *like* little children – not to *become* one (1 Corinthians 13:11). Jesus tells us to practice and awaken these child-like qualities within ourselves. It is through the wisdom of experience that these qualities manifest within us. To awaken these and similar qualities we have to want it. We are so caught up in this world and our intellectually stuffy perspectives, that nothing short of actually converting ourselves will enable us to let go and become as little children. When we are caught up, when we box the Spirit in with routines, habits, and social programming – the Spirit atrophies and disappears from our consciousness. The Path becomes a burden and religion becomes rigid dogma. Becoming like a child, seeing the world with fresh eyes, embracing what is before us, being enthusiastic and joyful, jumping in with all we got: that is what changes everything – that is the living Spirit flowing through us – that is how we enter Heaven.

Things to contemplate

"Verily I say unto you, except ye be converted, and become as little children, ye shall not enter unto the kingdom of heaven." (Matthew 18:2)
- What does converted mean?
- What does conversion have to do with becoming like a child?
- Is becoming like a child the only way into Heaven? Explain answer.

"Wherefore laying aside all malice, and all guile, and hypocrisies, and envies, and evil speaking. As newborns babes, desire the sincere milk of the word, that ye may grow thereby." (1 Peter 2:1)
- What is this verse saying?
- How does malice, guile, hypocrisies, envies, and evil speaking hinder growth?
- What is the "sincere milk of the word?"
- What characteristics of a child do you think Jesus was pointing to?

Practices to help awaken the child within

- Begin to see all things as Divine.
- Let things go.
- Say what's on your mind. Be truthful but avoid being hurtful!
- Do simple things like going to the park and staring at a flower, watch the clouds, or some other childish thing – see GOD's hand in everything.
- Be willing to play.
- Look at things with new eyes as if you have never seen them before.
- Be open to life and unknowing.
- Go play with kids.
- Let yourself go and stop taking yourself so seriously.
- Don't be so predictable.
- Stop being a know-it-all.
- Relax, enjoy, and be happy!

Faith

> *I say unto you, If ye have faith as a grain of a mustard seed, ye shall say unto this mountain, remove hence to yonder place; and it shall remove; and nothing shall be impossible unto you.* (Matthew 17:20)

Of course, when we have this deep faith we would never move a mountain because we know that all things are perfect just as they are. If this verse shows us anything, it's that not many people have this degree of faith.

Degrees of Faith:
- *Imitative* (An uninspired faith projected by someone to fit in or impress others)
- *Supported* (Faith upheld by the community, family, and friends)
- *Uncritical* (Non-judging faith that cannot be misdirected or confused: still some ignorance at this level)
- *Discovered* (Faith based on insights and understandings)
- *Mature* (Faith based on direct experience)

- *Longing* (Faith that seeks more experience)
- *Conviction* (Faith based on knowing and certainty)

Some factors that influence faith:
- Prayer
- Holy scriptures
- Inherited
- Taught
- Supernatural experiences and witnessing of real miracles
- It's what everyone believes
- Sounds rational
- Taught or shown to us by someone we respect and/or love
- Said to be true by people in power or authority
- Direct experience

There are hundreds of verses in the Bible that talk about faith. Some list qualities, others tell stories of people's faith, and still others highlight the differences between fruitful and unfruitful faith. It is essential to always remember that faith is the foundation of Christianity. Without it there is no direction, motivation, or hope of awakening the Christos. In Hebrews we are told that without faith there is no way to come to GOD.

> ***Without faith, it is impossible to please GOD: for they that cometh to GOD must believe that GOD is."***
> *(11:6)*

Through faith the Path of Christ awakens within us:

> *Add to your faith virtue; and to virtue knowledge; and to knowledge temperance; and to temperance patience; and to patience godliness; and to godliness brotherly kindness; and to brotherly kindness charity. For if these things be in you, and abound, they make you that ye shall neither be barren nor unfruitful. (2 Peter 1:5-8)*

While all these qualities are good, we are still told in James that:

> *Faith, if it hath not works, is dead, being alone.* (2:17)

If we have faith and fail to walk the Path Jesus showed us – then our faith is empty. We are told to believe, and if we really believed, we would do the work.

There are many degrees of faith: some people have little while others have the faith it takes to move mountains. We all have faith in something. If it is the fact that the world is round, that we are loved, or that we will not get hit by a drunk driver on the way to the store – all these things are taken on faith. The kind of faith that we are seeking as a Christians is to believe that Jesus showed us a way to GOD.

> *If any man will come after me, let him deny himself, and take up his cross and follow me.* (Matthew 16:23)

So how do we grow in faith? By doing the work, by walking the Path, by following in the footsteps of Jesus. In addition, we should surround ourselves with those that walk the Path, that follow the teachings of Jesus, and who embody the qualities of Christ within their lives. These things help us grow in faith.

Things to contemplate

"I say unto you, If ye have faith as a grain of a mustard seed, ye shall say unto this mountain, remove hence to yonder place; and it shall remove; and nothing shall be impossible unto you." (Matthew 17:20)

- Define faith.
- What does having faith mean to you?
- What are some of the signs of having faith?

"Without faith, it is impossible to please GOD: for they that cometh to GOD must believe that GOD is." (Hebrews 11:6)

- What is this verse saying?
- How is faith connected to belief?
- Can knowing replace faith? Why is faith so important?

"Add to your faith virtue; and to virtue knowledge; and to knowledge temperance; and to temperance patience; and to patience godliness; and to godliness brotherly kindness; and to brotherly kindness charity. For if these things be in you, and abound, they make you that ye shall neither be barren nor unfruitful." (2 Peter 1:5-8)
- Why must these things be added to faith?
- Are these qualities somehow related to faith or signs of faith?
- Can you not have these things and still be fruitful?

Faith, if it hath not works, is dead, being alone." (James 2:17)
- What is this verse saying?
- What are works?
- Are you taught to have more than faith? Explain.

"If any man will come after me, let him deny himself, and take up his cross and follow me." (Matthew 16:23)
- What does it mean deny yourself?
- How can you have a cross?
- In what way can you follow Jesus?
- What does it mean to follow? What actions can you do?

Practices to help grow faith
- Pray
- Read the scriptures and allow them to guide you.
- Allow some unknowing to arise in order to help create opportunities to have faith.
- Trust in yourself
    - That you are a good person
    - That you can walk the Path
    - That these practices will lead you down that Path
    - That you deserve to walk the Path
    - That Jesus would not have taught you to seek perfection if it were not possible
    - That you are a vessel for the Divine truth to manifest itself through

Thank You!

Chapter Six
Flowering Through Meditation

Meditation is not new age fluffy mental programming that ensnares the mind and takes us away from GOD, nor is it the invention of the eastern traditions or some esoteric yogic philosophy meant for a few crazy people. While meditation finds a place in each of these traditions, not one of them can claim it as theirs alone.

When reading the Bible we find that meditation has been practiced alongside prayer from the time of Isaac on up to our present day. One technique used by the Hebrews and Christians is a form of contemplation meditation which has the meditator repeatedly bring to mind the Laws of GOD and the teachings of Jesus until they have sunk deep within their heart.

This introduction is not intended to be an exhaustive treatment on meditative techniques, benefits, approaches, or paths. Instead, this introduction gives the reader enough information to practice and reap the benefits of their efforts. Below are some of the gifts we receive when we meditate with an open mind and sincere heart:

- Meditation stabilizes and calms the thought processes of the mind
- Meditation creates a peaceful space within to help us control our emotional reactions to life's stimuli
- It creates mindfulness of everything we do, say, and think
- It enables us to see our intentions and motivations more clearly
- Through calming the thoughts it invites tranquility
- It helps rid us of greed, desire, hatred, anger, attachments, and ignorance
- Opens us to the Divine
- Strengthens our relationship with the Spirit
- Deepens our understandings of the teachings
- Creates equanimity and joy
- And overall makes us more compassionate, patient, joyful, and content

There are hundreds of rules regarding the right techniques and/or edicts of meditation. While some of these rules help us meditate, many of them create a mystery around meditation that makes it difficult for the layperson to approach meditation without a guide. In a nutshell, meditation is nothing more than sitting down – and staying there.

Of course, some of the techniques were formulated to help us deal with the problems that arise when we just sit down and watch the mind do what it does. If we were to label the different practices of meditation and bring them all under two categories they would fall under Active or Passive Practices. The Passive Practices are considered a formal type of meditation where we sit down in a stable and still position and work with the mind. The Active Practices on the other hand can be done during any part of our day and primarily deal with being aware of what we are doing, saying, and thinking and/or being aware of the world around us. For the sake of this book we are only focusing on two passive forms of meditation.

The two forms of sitting meditation we will focus on are contemplation and concentration. Contemplation meditation takes on the characteristics of investigating a topic, recollecting holy verses, or working through issues in our lives via reflection. Concentration on the other hand deals with focusing on one thing in complete exclusion of all others. Different things we can use for this are simple visual references, sensations of the body, the sound, feeling and movement of the breath, a prayer or attribute of GOD, or any other single thing we can set awareness upon while the thoughts of the mind flow around our point of focus. The intent of concentrative meditation is to still the thinking mind and reach to that place within us where we connect with and awaken the Christos.

So now the question is: "How do we meditate?" Below are eighteen things to take into consideration as we begin to meditate. We should always keep in mind that the only thing needed for meditation is an aware mind - all the other stuff simply makes it easier to focus.

External
1. Sit facing a direction that has a calming and non-distractive effect on the mind
2. Avoid being in a space too constricting or too vast as to cause overwhelmingness
3. Be comfortable and secure
4. The air is to be clear and free of stagnation
5. The space is to be balanced, free from distractions, and in harmony with ones meditation
6. The belly should not be filled with food nor completely empty

Internal
1. Setting an intention
2. Create a Sacred Space within
3. Understanding what meditation is
4. Trusting and having faith in the Practice
5. Having a resolve to stick with the Practice no matter what
6. Being attentive, awake, and aware

Bodily Positions
1. As one sits the body is to be firm but relaxed, and the base should be stable and heavy
2. The back is straight, firm, relaxed, and pliable
3. The head is held up as if a string were pulling it from the middle of the crown
4. The arms are held off the ribs and the hands are positioned lightly on the lap or knees
5. Eyelids are loose and relaxed and the eyes are soft and pointed down at a thirty-degree angle.
6. The tongue is placed lightly on the roof of the mouth behind the front teeth. This helps slow down the saliva glands and connect the two polarities of the body.

Now it is time to sit down and meditate! We can read all we want, but unlike literary or scientific knowledge, you haven't learned anything about meditation until you do it. Set aside some time every day for meditation. At first set aside fifteen minutes – or just five minutes if that is all you have to give. Once the time has been set, be consistent and make an effort to sit down at that time and meditate every day. Beyond the fact that we are creatures of habit, the more we meditate the easier it becomes. After a few weeks we notice the mind slowing down, we are better able to focus and remember things, our thought processes are clear, and we begin to have control over the thoughts and emotions. The most important thing with meditation is to do it. So do it!

The five degrees of concentration meditation:
1. *Applied thought:* Directing or focusing the mind upon something.
2. *Sustained thought:* Maintaining the focus of the mind.
3. *Joyfulness:* A feeling that arises when the mind has stabilized and the sensory experiences dissolve into the background.
4. *Bliss:* A state of being when the mind has retained a continued focus on the object. At this level an exchange of energy occurs between the meditator and object of focus.
5. *Rapture:* State of union when the object and subject have become one.

These five levels or degrees of meditation give us an idea of what to expect when we begin to meditate. So now let us get to it.

Contemplation Meditation

This one is the easiest thing to do. Sit down and think. First bring to mind a verse. I will pick one randomly from the Four Gospels to use as an example:

> *Leave there thy gift before the altar, and go thy way; first be reconciled to thy brother, and then come and offer thy gift. (Matthew 5:24)*

Now that we have the verse, next we need to consider what level of the verse we are to meditate on. Traditionally there are five ways to investigate a sacred teaching:

1. Literal
2. Symbolic
3. Metaphorical

4. Numerological
5. Secretive

Literally this verse is telling us to leave our gift before the altar and deal with the troubles we have with others before giving our offering.

Symbolically we can look at this verse in a million different ways – this is one of the signs and characteristics of Holy Writing. So many Christians get into conflict because there are an infinite number of ways to read into a scripture. The very first thing we need to do when we are breaking something down symbolically is to understand our own symbolism. Taking this verse as a base to work from, the first thing we need to do is take the key words out. In this case we have leave, gift, altar, reconcile, and brother. What do these words mean to you? To me leave represents a sense of separation. It is often associated with running away or a situation that brings relief or sadness. Altar brings to mind the sacred, a place where all of our understandings of creation are symbolically represented. It is the foundation of our practices. It is where we place our sacred objects, images, and prayers upon. Gift on the other hand invokes an idea of giving something to another. There are superficial gifts and then there are gifts that come from the heart. In this case, the gift represents to me a giving of ourselves. The word reconcile means many things to me, one of which is finding a state of balance. Lastly, the word brother conjures up the idea of everyone and everything in my life. So symbolically this verse is telling me that i must find a balance within my life and seek peace with all my relations before my offering will be received.

Metaphorically we are shown that our gifts are empty until we have found peace within our lives. The only real gift we can give to GOD, the only thing we really have to offer is ourselves. Not our bodies, for they will disintegrate and return to the earth, and not our minds, because they were never ours in the first place. We cannot offer anything physical, because it is already GOD's. The only things we can offer are our words, actions, and thoughts. The only sure way to do this is to walk as Jesus taught us, and a part of that walk is to forgive others and to act through compassion.

Numerologically there is no logical way to decipher a holy verse unless it is in the original language: such as Hebrew or Greek. And the Secret understandings that lay hidden within sacred scriptures come through revelation and embodiment of the teachings.

Breaking down scriptures is one way to use contemplation meditation. Another way is to simply meditate on our actions, our life, the things that we do that are helpful or harmful to our Christian Path, the qualities of Christ, the good things we wish to invite into our lives, different understandings of the scriptures, or anything else that we can think of. The idea behind contemplation is to find something that is wholesome and beneficial to our Path, and then simply meditate upon it until it has saturated our minds and entered our hearts.

Concentration Meditation

In comparison to contemplation meditation, learning to concentrate and hold our focus on one thing in exclusion of all others is very difficult. One reason for this is that contemplation is an active practice that leads the mind while concentration merely seeks to rest the mind upon a chosen focus. When we rest the mind we find that our thoughts, emotions, feelings, sensory impressions that surround us at all times, and the memories imbedded in our cells and neurons are constantly in motion and beyond our control to stop. In fact, the harder we try to stop them, the more powerful they become. The longer we sit motionless and focused, the harder it is to do so. This, above any other reason, is a good motivation for learning how to concentrate. If we cannot control what thoughts, images, and emotions flow through us, how can we ever hope to aspire to follow in the footsteps of Jesus?

There are as many things to concentrate upon as there are thoughts. The idea behind concentration meditation is not to focus upon a million things in one minute, but to focus on one thing for a million minutes. It does not matter what it is that we focus upon; the only stipulation might be to consider focusing on things that are positive and productive towards awakening compassion and wholesomeness. It would not serve us to focus on an image of a naked person, especially if we are trying to avoid lustfulness. But even this rule can be broken if it helps us sever our attachments to desire.

What needs to be emphasized is that whatever we choose to focus on, we are to remain with that one thing until the benefits of concentrative meditation have born forth. There are many levels, degrees, gifts, and powers that come to us when we go deeper into concentrative meditation. While these gifts and powers can arise, it is important to keep our focus on the Path. Our intention for meditation should bring us closer to awakening the Christos within, not for gaining supernatural powers that allow us to see through walls, leap tall buildings, or fly faster than the speed of sound. Meditation is a real practice that has real results when we apply ourselves to doing it. The potential of gaining powers should never be the focus of our efforts. Our focus should always be directed towards the Path and to awakening the Christos.

The example we are going to use to show the process of concentrative meditation is an image of the cross. We are not going to get crazy and start visualizing Jesus on the cross or some cross highlighted upon a mountain of skulls, blood dripping from it, or any other elaborate imagery. We are going to visualize a simple wooden cross. Nothing more and nothing less!

Having found a comfortable seat in a conducive place for meditation, we lightly close our eyes and begin to visualize. For some this might be hard to do. One way to overcome this is to have a picture or an actual cross to stare at before we close our eyes so as to help us retain the image. What we find when we close our eyes is that this simple image is not easy to visualize much less retain as a focus for any amount of time. We should remember as we go into this process that what we visualize is not going to be as concrete as what we see with our eyes – at least for the beginner. The reason for this is based upon the way we are bringing this information into consciousness. With that in mind, we needn't worry about the image being the same as when we see it with our eyes. As our meditation grows we find the visualization becoming more real and intense then when looking at it through our eyes. For now do not be discouraged if what you see has little tangibility.

So what do you see? Can you actually retain a ghost of its shape or can you see it as clear as day? Does the image fluctuate and seek to form into something else or might it be turning and floating as if seeking to go out of focus? Any and all of these things can happen. Other things that will most likely happen is that you will forget what you are doing. Thoughts might come and go and you might find yourself floating along with them. While this happens, what we are to do is gently bring our focus back to the cross. The point is not to judge ourselves, our thoughts, or anything else for that matter. What we need to do is simply let go of all thoughts, images, emotions, and feelings, and bring our focus back to the cross.

It is not easy – but it can be done. That is what we need to remember as we bring our attention away from some horrible thought for the thousandth time. It is amazing how scary and messed up the thoughts can be that float through our awareness. Most, if not all of them, are merely images we have acquired from movies and television. Sometimes we find ourselves rehearsing something that happened a long time ago or daydreaming about the future. We might rehearse our day or have amazing insights into the nature of the universe. Once again, all that we need to do is bring our focus back to the cross.

Concentration in principle is not that difficult. In practice, it is one of the most difficult things we do on the Path. These minds are filled with so much information, that to even dream of stilling them is a dream within a dream. It is possible though.

So here we are again bringing the focus back to the cross. It is not thoughts now that distract us; it is an excruciating pain in our leg, an itch on the shoulder, a lobbing head or slouching back. It is the body that seeks to get up from this uncomfortable place and walk around. While it is natural for the body to seek relief, know that during a three hour movie when the mind is completely ensnared in the story, not once does the it get achy or seek to move around least the attention become broken and the movie loses a little of its escapists power. If the body gets so uncomfortable that it causes us to lose our focus, then simply readjust with the minimal effort to avoid bringing our minds out of the calm state it is in. Sometimes taking our attention from the cross and focusing it on the pain for a minute or two will often have the result of releasing the mind from the pain itself. Although this seems a little strange, in practice it works.

Another way the body creates distraction is to make the mind obsess over the saliva in the throat or challenge our meditation with bodily needs. To minimize this problem make sure you go to the bathroom before meditation, avoid eating or drinking things that create phlegm and gas, and eat just enough to satiate the stomach but not fill it up before meditation.

The next thing that might come up is sensory distractions. Maybe it is a flash of light that strikes the eyelids, a loud sound down the street, or the temperature of the room. All these things and many more come and rob us of our Practice. We can control only a few of these things. There are three ways to deal with these distractions. We can give up and allow our attention to waver. We can fight the distraction like a drill sergeant and hold to our chosen focus like a dog to a stick, or we can temporarily shift our focus to the momentary distraction and try to be as aware and attentive to the sound, light, or whatever other distraction it is as we were with our chosen focus. We do this until the distraction has gone and we notice that our minds are clinging to the memory of the distraction rather than the actual event. When we notice our minds clinging to the memory we shift our focus back to our chosen visualization. This last approach is the healthiest way to integrate life's randomness into our Practice.

Now let's talk about some things that can happen during meditation. Some of these things might or might not ever happen. The point in mentioning them is to prepare you just in case they do. When we sit for a long time in one position the body can do a lot of odd things. Some of these consist of random temperature changes, profuse sweating, twitching, vibrating, or even hopping around like a body that is half asleep and then suddenly jerks awake. Other things that can happen are hearing loud sounds, feeling excruciating pain as if being pierced by thorns, seeing phantoms or ghostly images, and the sensation of levitating. All we need to do is bring our focus back to the cross. We can argue for or against these things being real. Their validity is not the point; bringing our focus back to the cross is all that matters. If on the other hand we find ourselves becoming overwhelmed with these sensations then take a moment to focus on them. When we bring our attention to these ethereal sensations we should use the moment to let go. When we can truly let go these fears and obsessions will dissipate on their own. All that we need to do then is bring our focus back to the cross.

As our ability to retain this image grows we find ourselves more at peace with our surroundings, in greater control over our thoughts, and having a clearer vision of life. On top of that, we begin to experience the joy, bliss, and rapture that was spoken of earlier in this chapter. The ability to stay focused and aware enables us to help others because we can see clearly - we have taken the beam out of our own eye (Matthew 7:5). On top of that, the unwholesome emotions and thoughts that use to plague us incessantly before have dissolved and in their place is a mind which is wholesome, loving, compassionate, and awake. It is at this point that we really begin to understand the benefits of meditation. So meditate often!

Chapter Seven
The Harvest: Awakening Compassion Within

> *A certain man went down from Jerusalem to Jericho, and fell among thieves, which stripped him of his raiment, and wounded him, and departed, leaving him half dead. And by chance there came down a certain priest that way: and when he saw him, he passed by on the other side. And likewise a Levite, when he was at the place, came and looked on him, and passes by on the other side. But a certain Samaritan, as he journeyed, came where he was, and when he saw him, he had compassion on him. And went to him, and bound up his wounds, pouring in oil and wine, and set him on his own beast, and brought him to an inn, and took care of him. And on the morrow when he departed, he took out two pence, and gave them to the host, and said unto him, take care of him; and whatsoever thou spendest more, when I come again, I will repay thee. Which now of these three, thinkest thou, was neighbor unto him that fell among the thieves? And he said, He that showed mercy on him. Then said Jesus unto him, go do thou likewise."* (Luke 10:30-37)

Compassion is not a word we should use lightly. As we see above, it is an act that opens hearts and silences minds: those with compassion are truly Divine.

The basic principle of Awakening Compassion is simple: we take upon ourselves the pain and suffering of the world and send back love, joy, health, and wellness. Awakening Compassion is the pinnacle of the Christian teachings. Sadly, it is not something we find often in life.

Christianity has many compassionate qualities. It is a religion known for feeding and giving clothes, warmth, shelter, and love. All these qualities show that Christianity breeds compassionate action. And yet, there is something missing. While there are many Christians who are genuinely compassionate, what we most often find is money given out of guilt, pressure, pleasure, fear, and/or desire. While this money is channeled to good causes, the problem is that compassion is not a disconnected practice. It gets dirty, feels the pain, relates with the pain, and seeks to uplift those who suffer by taking their pain and suffering away. Compassion is a practice that comes from the heart not the mind or wallet.

The following Compassion practice can be formal or spontaneous. The formal practice begins with the preparatory stages of meditation in chapter six and then follows the sequence as laid out below. The spontaneous practice happens whenever there is a situation that is uncomfortable in our lives or when we see a situation that is painful, harmful, or unhealthy to ourselves or others. The major difference between the formal and spontaneous practice is the initial intensity of the emotions involved.

Stages of Compassion Meditation

- Create an open space for the Spirit to flow through us
- Connect with the emotions and let go of the story line
- Personalizing it by doing the practice for oneself and those close at heart
- Do the meditation for strangers and enemies

Creating an open space

> *He breathed on them, and saith unto them, Receive ye the Holy Ghost. (John 20:22)*

As we sit down to meditate we should calm our minds and focus on our breath in order to create an open space to connect with the Spirit. The space we create is free from attachments, desires, judgments, fears, and conceptions.

To create an open space we sit down as instructed in chapter six and focus all of our attention on the breath. Direct the consciousness to sink into the breath, while at the same time allowing all thoughts, feelings, and images to dissolve into the emptiness of the mind. If this non-conceptual practice is too difficult then consciously visualize an infinite space such as the ocean, outer space, the sky, or some limitless field and make the mind reside in this place until a sense of peace and openness has awakened within.

Connecting and letting go

Often in life we find ourselves running away from the uncomfortable feelings that arise. We cling to the storyline and feed it with thoughts and emotions instead of letting go of the situation and experiencing what is going on inside of us in the moment. It is as if we have been stabbed in the chest and instead of tending our wound, we chase after the assailant. By chasing after the attacker, we are killing instead of healing ourselves.

The storyline represents our subjective perception of whatever situation arises within our lives. If it happens that the given situation is undesirable, we will externalize our feelings and emotions so that it is easier to deal with. Of course, there are always those who internalize their feelings to make it worse for themselves, but as a general rule, most of us will externalize our internal issues to avoid being vulnerable.

By connecting with our emotions and feelings we can divert our mind from creating a whole reality based upon our perceptions and memories of what happened. By avoiding this trap, we create an opportunity to work on healing the wounds that invite unfruitful and harmful emotions into our lives.

Personalizing the practice

We have created an open space, let go of the storyline, and connected with the feeling, now we begin the practice of Awakening Compassion. Connect with the feeling deeply, open up to it without judgment or aversion. Next, dissolve it into the heart and send yourself whatever good feelings or things you can think of. Sometimes it might be a white light, while other times it might be a feeling of love and endearment, a picture of a flower, or some memory that brought great joy into your life.

Take the unwanted feeling and convert it into love. By doing this, we are taking away the world's suffering and sending out joy in its place. This is hard because it is scary and difficult to open up to suffering – it is even more difficult to take it into our hearts. Some of us might believe we do not deserve love or happiness. These are thoughts and feelings that hold us back from being compassionate. How can we send love to others when we cannot even send it to ourselves?

The idea of this practice is to exchange loss with union, hate with love, despair with hope, and whatever other dichotomous relationship we find that deals with unwholesome experiences and feelings verses nourishing ones. It is possible to do this – because we can do it.

Now a question might arise that challenges the validity of doing this practice in the first place. What good does it really do? To answer this all that needs to be said is that it does not hurt or make things worse. In fact, while it might or might not stop us from having these feelings in the moment, it does invite other feelings to arise. Although it is not an action that affects a situation directly, it is a thought that can trigger a healthy reaction instead of a harmful and hurtful one. We would be hard press to find someone who could reasonably argue that good thoughts are a bad thing, or for that matter, a waste of time.

Logically we might have a hard time finding some ground to argue the value of this practice. In fact, logic would definitely tell us that taking in bad things and sending out good ones would most likely deplete us of all good things. We should hoard our riches and all the good things while throwing away the trash. That is logical thinking. In practice though, what we find is the complete opposite. By hoarding the good we create separation, darkness, and suffering; while sending out good thoughts we promote a healthier environment filled with joy, sharing, and abundance. And who better to start with then ourselves?

After we have done this taking and giving with ourselves, we shift our focus to those we love. To our children, parents, siblings, grandparents, friends, and whoever else falls into this category. We do the same meditation. Only this time, we recognize that they have felt this same emotion at one time or another, and so we take their pain and suffering from them. We take that feeling into our heart and transform it into love before sending it back to them. If the feeling is pain because of some physical ailment, then we take the pain and send them health and comfort. If the emotion is fear, then we take the fear and send them comfort and strength. Whatever the initial feeling we begin the meditation with, we now recognize that those we love have also been afflicted by the same feeling and so we free them of it.

Can we actually take away the pain, fear, worry, and loss from others? Who knows? The point of this practice is to open us to Compassion. If it has good results in the external world, then so much the better. Ultimately this practice is to open our hearts and minds to love, kindness, and compassion. One thing is for certain, the more we do this practice, the greater patience, perseverance, joy, open-heartedness, non-judgmentalness, and other Christ qualities arise within our lives.

Universalizing

Taking the pain and suffering and transforming it for ourselves and those we love is relatively simple to do. Taking and transforming it for people we do not know or those who actually wish us harm is a whole different story.

> **But I say unto you. Love your enemies, bless them that curse you, do good to them that hate you, and pray for them which despitefully use you, and persecute you.** *(Matthew 5:44)*

Now that is hard!

The practice is exactly the same as when we did it for those we love. Everyone has similar feelings – the storyline and intensity might be different, but the suffering is the same. For we have all felt loss, pain, hatred, fear, anxiety, and on and on. First do the practice for those we do not know and then do it for our enemies.

We all want love, happiness, and abundance. Some of us seek it in strange and round-about ways, but in the end, even the drug dealer, murderer, or thief wants to be happy. While it is hard to send love to those who have hurt us, it truly helps us heal our internal wounds. It might not make the other person better, but it makes us better and it brings in a greater peace then when we hold onto our frustrations, animosities, and hatred. We are told to first make amends with our neighbor before we bring our offering to the altar. We must see that to enter into heaven, we need to let go of suffering.

Ending with a Bang

What is there to say? If you practice what Jesus taught, you will find joy and abundance. It is possible – for why would he tell us to do something impossible? There are a million things we can talk about, but in the end, the only thing that needs to be said is read and practice what is in this book.

Do not look at me as a saint, nor for that matter as a true Christian. I lust, get angry, have a hard time being patient, want to be rich, desire material possessions, do not want to work, have a hard time with judgmentalness, rarely dedicate anything i do to GOD, many of my actions are selfish, i have a lot of attachments, what faith i boast is often misplaced, and on and on i can go about myself and my unworthiness. If you use me as a gauge to judge this book – it will fall short every time.

I am not a good example! In fact, prior to finishing this text i debated about writing it at all. Who am i to talk about Jesus and his teachings? The only reason why i continued is that i could do nothing less than give my life over to the Divine and this writing has become my dedication.

The original motivation for writing this book was to create a solid path for me to walk on. I have had a difficult time finding my way into the teachings of Jesus because i never found a person or writing that could direct me towards what can been done to embody his wisdom. While church is inspirational and supportive, it rarely offers a practical approach to applying the teachings of Jesus, much less show us how to awaken the Christos. There is always inspiring stories, personal understandings of the scriptures, a weekly lesson/reflection to consider, some homework, and some fellowship at the end, but when it is all said and done, the inspiration fades away, the lessons get lost in our day-to-day life, and the fellowship turns into maybe a Bible study once a week or a night of poker and drinking beers.

My problem stemmed from what I had been taught and what I saw versus what Jesus tells us to do. We go to church once a week, read the scriptures, and maybe do something nice for those in need. Where is the practice? To become a doctor we have to go to school, learn what needs to be learned, help those who are sick, and practice a lot before we have the right to call ourselves a doctor. How much more difficult is it to be a true Christian. The truth is, it takes a lot more work, practice, and dedication to become a Christian. We think dunking our heads in water and believing that Jesus died for our sins is all that it takes. This text represents what i believe to be the first step towards becoming a Christian: one who has awoken the Christos. May this writing be a support to those who seek as i do! GOD Bless.

Sincerely,

A Follower of Christ

AMEN

Appendix I
One Year Study Plan

If done in a group or Bible study format have the participants read and do the journaling before talking about the subject. This ensures there will be lively talks, discussions, and exchanges every week. If there is no specific direction, then read each section, answer the questions, and do the practices as you see fit. Take your time. There is no rush, no golden star, and nobody looking over your shoulder making sure you do it. This is for you – so do it right!

1. Read text and write what you think ☐
2. Preciousness of Life ☐
3. Impermanence ☐
4. Reaping what we Sow: Actions ☐
5. Reaping what we Sow: Speech ☐
6. Reaping what we Sow: Thoughts ☐
7. Narrowness of the Path ☐
8. Poorness ☐
9. Mourning ☐
10. Meekness ☐
11. Hungering and Thirsting ☐
12. Merciful ☐
13. Purity of Heart ☐
14. Peacemaker ☐
15. Persecuted ☐
16. Being Focused ☐
17. Being Content ☐
18. Being free of Jealousy ☐
19. Being free of Judgments towards Others ☐
20. Being free of Judgments towards Ourselves ☐
21. Being free of Expectations ☐
22. Being Joyful ☐
23. Being Sacred ☐

24. Knowledge
25. Virtue: questions and practices
26. Virtue: self study
27. Giving: questions and practices
28. Giving: internal and external
29. Patience: questions and practices
30. Patience: three examples of patience
31. Perseverance
32. Temperance: questions and answers
33. Temperance: restraint and self control
34. Temperance: balance and harmony
35. Humbleness: questions and practices
36. Humbleness: pray, fast, and silence
37. Kindness
38. Tranquility
39. Wisdom
40. Adversity: questions and practices
41. Adversity: 2nd week questions and practices
42. Become like a child
43. Faith: questions and practices
44. Faith: go over specifics
45. Meditation: concentration meditations
46. Meditation: contemplation meditations
47. Read chapter seven and write down thoughts
48. Do for self
49. Do for self, loved ones, and friends
50. Do for self, friends, loved ones, and others
51. Do complete set
52. Read diary – assess growth. Was it worth it?

Weeks four, five, and six: Reaping What We Sow

Week four

- Answer the questions that go with this section and do the practices.

- Take a physical item that you covet and give it to someone.
- Re-pay something that was either intentionally or inadvertently taken. If it was a pen or lighter, then give one to the person you took it from. If it was some paper from the copy machine at work, replace it with a whole packet of paper. If a piece of candy at the grocery store – either pay for one and return it or leave a quarter at those toy machines at the entrance of the store. The idea of this practice is not to bring attention to what you have done, but simply to bring the attention to yourself and balance it.
- Make a list of all the actions you have done this week that were not conducive to your Path.
- Research violence: write about the feelings, intentions, reasons, and justifications a person might have for harming another. Are they in control, is this what they want, might this be how they were treated? Come up with as many different questions as possible. Then do the same for the victim. Once you have a basic idea of the situation, think about what led to the violence and what happened afterwards. Then consider violence on a grand scale. First with groups, then move on to political and religious wars, etc... What is the root of violence? What emotions are related to violence? What thoughts?

Week five

- Answer the questions that go with this section and do the practices.
- For twenty-four hours say only those things that are absolutely necessary to get on with your day. If possible, say nothing.
- Listen at work, school, at home, and at parties: what are people saying?

- If you have a recorder, record everything you say today. If you do not have a recorder, try to write down the basic conversations you had. If nothing else, at least listen to what you say. Do you slander, gossip, lie, or speak offensively to others? Why? What purpose does it serve?
- What is the feeling you get when someone is lying to you?
- Make a list of all the different reasons people lie? Examples: reputation, protecting themselves, showing off, etc...
- Think about tone of voice, intention of speaking, and the way you say things. How do these effect/affect others?
- What is the purpose of speech?

Week six

- Answer the questions that go with this section and do the practices.
- How many verses talk about "no thought?" No thought for what you eat, drink, wear, et cetera – and no thought for what to say or do. How is premeditation and thought connected with your will?
- In other verses Jesus highlights the merit of thought when he asks his disciples, "What think thee?" This dual nature of thinking is very important. In one regard you are to avoid worrying or feeding your thoughts with fears and desires. On the other hand, Jesus emphasizes the importance of using reason to understand the teachings. While the nature of reason has merit, Jesus points to an even greater level of understanding in Matthew 16:17 and other such verses that talk about how the revealed truth is the highest knowledge attainable unto man. This wisdom does not come from objective knowledge and subjective

perceptions but from the direct experience of the Divine within.
- There are many verses that connect the heart with thoughts. What is Matthew 15:8 saying? Why are your thoughts so important? How is thinking connected with the heart in the Gospels? Give a few examples.
- When you find yourself having trouble dealing with some thoughts try to use the polarity technique. Most thoughts have their opposite. When you are thinking badly towards something, work on having good thoughts in its place. Instead of angry thoughts, try joyful ones – hateful thoughts, loving ones. This does not mean you have to think lovingly towards someone you hate – just have loving thoughts towards someone you love. It is hard to have hate in your heart when love is there. The point is, to use the opposing thought process to dissolve the unwanted ones.

Weeks nineteen and twenty: Judging

Week twenty

- Answer the questions that go with this section and do the practices.
- Become aware of your judgments by writing down every one you have in each of the following categories:
    1. At other people
    2. At animals
    3. Family and friends
    4. Bums on the street
    5. People with disabilities
    6. Uneducated people or intellectuals
    7. Rich or poor
    8. Pets or the meat that some of us eat
    9. Pintos and Mercedes

10. Music, literature, and movies
11. Smells and sights
12. Conversations
13. Political and religious viewpoints
14. The way people dress and carry themselves
15. What people spend their money on
16. Children in general
17. Parenting
18. Age, color, sex, and race
19. Etc...

- How do these judgments affect you?
- Go through each judgment and find its root. Do you agree with it? Did you ever agree with it?
- Figure out which judgments no longer hold sway and do positive affirmations to change them. *Example:* A judgment of a mundane conversation that has no value but to fill in space. *Affirmation:* "In all conversations there is something to gain." By doing this you are transforming judgments into a way of growing and being open to the Spirit of the moment.

Week twenty-one

- Become aware of your self-judgments by writing down every one you have in the following categories:
    1. Your body
    2. Your relationships
    3. Your children
    4. Your parents
    5. Your siblings
    6. Your emotions
    7. Your thoughts
    8. Your beliefs
    9. Your public and private self
    10. Your upbringing
    11. Who you are in general

Appendix I: One Year Study Plan

    12. Your efforts
    13. Your stamina
    14. Your education or understandings
    15. Your weaknesses
    16. Your strengths
    17. Your abilities
    18. Your sexual performance
    19. Etc...

- Go through the same process that you went through with others.
- Do self-judgments benefit you? Really?
- Why is the following verse unique in religious history: "Judge not, that ye be not judged"? How is this a paradigm shift from the Old Testament?
- What is the difference between judging and discerning?

Weeks twenty-five and twenty-six: Virtue

Week twenty-five

- Answer the questions that go with this section and do the practices.
- Learn about two other cultural, religious, or philosophical systems of virtue. What is different about them and what is the same?
- Do a confession by considering your whole life and writing down the key moments in your life that you regret because of non-virtuous actions. If tears come, so much the better. Be authentic and truthful.

Week Twenty-six

- Look at each of these non-virtuous actions below and write three different times you have done them. If you are not able to remember or unable to write or even think about them, it is okay. Just remember to check in with this practice once in a while to see if you are ready to deal with whatever it is or was. For those who are pure or who for some blessed reason have not done one or more of these acts – be thankful.

1. Causing physical harm to others
2. Greed
3. Stealing
4. Sexual misconduct
5. Slandering
6. Insulting
7. Lying
8. Deception
9. Gossip
10. Derogatory or offensive speech
11. Judging
12. Egotistical pride
13. Idleness
14. Gluttony
15. Coveting
16. Debauchery and drunkenness
17. Sacrilege
18. Flattery and manipulation
19. Mistreating and using others
20. Mistrusting
21. Failing to give when given the chance
22. Making excuses
23. Missing sacred moments
24. Ingratitude
25. Impure thoughts
26. Not being open and aware
27. Thinking bad thoughts about others
28. Critiquing others to the point of attacking
29. Avoidance or ignoring
30. Neglecting people or responsibilities
31. Unbalanced anger
32. Not listening

33. Come up with a few of your own
- Write down the virtuous qualities you embody now.
- Make a list of all the virtues and qualities you wish to embody.
- How do you become virtuous? What things can you do to invite these virtuous qualities into your life?

Weeks twenty-seven and twenty-eight: Giving

Week twenty-seven

- Answer the questions that go with this section and do the practices.
- Make a list of all the things you have been given in life. Consider the list below when thinking about what you have received.
   1. Parents
   2. Family
   3. Siblings
   4. Friends
   5. Intimate relationships
   6. Neighbors
   7. Strangers
   8. Enemies
   9. Teachers
   10. Companions
   11. Pets
   12. Church
   13. Work
   14. Organizations
   15. Movies
   16. Books
   17. Education
   18. Experiences
   19. Nature

20. Wild animals
21. Objects
22. Games
23. Meditation
24. Prayer
25. Adventures
26. GOD
27. Etc…

Week twenty-eight

- Make a list of the different reason you give.
- Take three things from the list of external giving and do them.
- Take three things from the list of internal giving and do them.
- As you work with giving make sure to consider the five factors of giving. What is your intention? How are you giving: to be seen, talked about, or secretly? Who are you giving to? Do they really need these things or is this simply a way of doing the practice without going out of your way? What is it you are giving? Is it something that is really needed? What is your viewpoint? Take all these things into consideration as you do this practice.

Weeks twenty-nine and thirty: Patience

Week twenty-nine

- Answer the questions that go with this section and do the practices.
- Write down all the ways you have been patient this week.
- Write down how you reacted when your patience was tested.

- Give three examples on how each of these different areas give you an opportunity to practice patience.
  1. Effort
  2. Time
  3. Tribulations
  4. Interactions
  5. Strangers
  6. Children
  7. Animals
  8. Communicating
  9. Driving
  10. Technology
  11. Goals
  12. Educations
  13. Personal ability
  14. Family
  15. Making money
  16. Waiting in line
  17. Relationships
  18. Entertainment
  19. Employment
- Write down the different feelings, thoughts, and emotions that arise when you become impatient. Also recognize your breathing. Is it sharp, relaxed, long, short, etc? How about your heartbeat?

Week Thirty

- How can you be patient and still not tolerate something?
- Describe how patience can be physical, mental, and emotional. Can you have only one or two of these and still be patient?
- Are you more patient with some people and situations and not others? Name a few examples.

- Are you more patient with those you love or with strangers? Explain answer.
- Make a list of all the things you are patient with.
- Make a list of the things you want to be patient with.
- Take one particular situation or person you want to be patient with and roll play a scenario of the situation with which you wish to exhibit patience in. By doing this often you are conditioning yourself to be patient. Do this practice with other situations as well.

Weeks thirty-two, thirty-three, and thirty-four: Temperance

Week thirty-two

- Answer the questions that go with this section and do the practices.
- Make a list of all the things that trigger unwanted emotions, thoughts, and actions.
- Work on avoiding those situations or arranging things so that these situations do not come up.

Week thirty-three

- With the list of things that trigger unwanted emotions, thoughts, and actions: memorize a Biblical verse for each temptation. Every time the temptation comes up, allow the verse to come to mind. Let the verse burn away all thoughts, emotions, and desires for action.
- Create a list of things you can do when temptations arises. Implement when needed.
- Use prayer as a means to overcome desire. Whenever the temptation arises call upon GOD to help you. Open yourself to GOD's strength. This type of prayer needs to be with all your heart and all your mind.

Week thirty-four

- Describe what balance would look like in your life.
- Define what self-control is.
- Make a list of all the unbalanced things in your life.
- With that list write what things you can do to bring balance.
- Define balance when it comes to focusing on material and spiritual things.
- How can you create harmony with others when your beliefs differ from theirs? Make a list of the different things that you can do.

Week thirty-five and thirty-six: Humbleness

Week thirty-five

- Answer the questions that go with this section and do the practices.
- Create opportunities to practice humility.
- Make a list of all the characteristics a humble person exhibits.

Week thirty-six

- Pray and meditate every day and continue for the rest of your life.
- Refrain from talking for at least a few hours in the day. Try a whole day if you can.
- Fast at least once this week. Levels of fasting:
    1. Avoid eating or drinking certain things during a designated time
    2. No food for six hours
    3. No food from sunup to sundown

4. No food for twenty-four hours
- Constantly check yourself to see if you are feeling inflated.
- Avoid being praised and avoid looking for recognition.
- Dedicate yourself completely to the Path.
- Constantly be thankful.
- When you practice anoint yourself, splash your face, and never show the world you are practicing.
- Take the lesser portion, let the last go, take the lesser seat, allow people to speak, let go!

Weeks forty and forty-one: Adversity

Week forty

- Answer the questions that go with this section and do the practices.
- Write down how your past actions have created your present experiences.
- Read Job and write down why he suffered so much.
- Why did the Prodigal Son have to go away?
- Consider the suffering Jesus experienced.
- Reflect on what Christian practices you can work on during different temptations.
- Allow temptation to motivate you on the Path.
- Use adversity to wake up.
- Take the moment to relate to the suffering of others.
- Consider a life without suffering and what motivation would there be to become a Christian without it?

Week forty-one

- How do you deal with pain and tribulations?

- What temptations right now are you just not ready to work with?
- What things in your life right now create opportunities to practice?
- Begin to consciously confront issues in your life?
- Work with positive affirmations to support your efforts.
- Pray to GOD for support and help with those things you cannot work with on your own.
- Write down five different verses in the Bible that show you how to deal with adversity?
- Anytime you find yourself unbalanced, consider which of the practices in this text apply to your situation and then do the practice.

Week forty-three and forty-four: Faith

Week forty-three

- Answer the questions that go with this section and do the practices.
- Contemplate five different verses dealing with faith.
- What is your level of faith?
    1. Imitative (An uninspired faith projected by someone to fit in or impress others)
    2. Supported (Faith upheld by the community, family, and friends)
    3. Uncritical (Non-judging faith that cannot be misdirected or confused – still some ignorance at this level)
    4. Discovered (Faith based on insights and understandings)
    5. Mature (Faith based off of direct experience)
    6. Longing (Faith grown from experience and which seeks more experience)

7. Conviction (Faith based on knowing and certainty)
- Describe how you grow in faith.
- What brought you to Christianity? Are those factors still alive and growing?

Week forty-four

- Does faith have to be based on truth? Can we not have faith in things that are false?
- What level of faith would you say most Christians are coming from?
- Do you need others to believe?
- Is faith and blind faith the same thing?
- Does faith have to be logical?
- When can faith be harmful?
- Is science and religion injurious to each other? Explain.
- Does the Bible have to be historically accurate in order for your faith to have solid ground to stand upon?

Appendix II
Secondary Practices: Going the Extra Mile

- Anger
- Love
- Forgiveness
- Prayer

These secondary practices are the winter's harvest. While they are found throughout this text, it never hurts to look at things a little deeper. Anger is something that affects all of us. For some it might be a trifling annoyance while for others it could be a big problem. One of the most powerful tools we have to combat anger and hatred is love. Love is the antidote while forgiveness is the natural result of that love.

Prayer has been added to this appendix because it was never touched upon in the text. One reason for this is that most Christians have at least an elementary knowledge of prayer and its uses. The intention of adding it to this appendix is simply for wholeness sake. No book on Christianity would be complete without at least touching prayer.

Anger

> ***For the wrath of man worketh not the righteousness of God.*** *(James 1:20)*

Nothing is more harmful to mental peace and serenity than anger and hatred. While there are many justifications, excuses, and uses for anger, in the end it unbalances us, and in extreme cases, causes us and others harm. Those who fall prey to anger often look at it as the fault of their environment or the people around them. Many believe they are victims because they are powerless and have no control over it. While this is the foremost excuse some others are:

- Righteous anger
- They deserve it
- That is just what happens
- That is just who I am
- Keeps us from being taken advantage of
- Saves us when we are afraid
- Protects us when we are vulnerable
- Morally justified
- Motivates us to deal with situations or undertake unwanted tasks
- Causes others to fear and avoid us
- Forces others to do what we want
- Gives us a neurochemical rush that relieves anxiety and provides a physiological boost
- We are addicted to it
- Inherited
- Alcohol or some other drug
- That is the only way they will listen
- That is the only way they will learn
- It helps others
- It gets things done
- It relieves internal tension
- It is a habit

As we see above, anger can be justified in many ways. While sometimes it has positive results, in most cases it leaves in its wake feelings of hurt and pain, anxiety and restlessness, separation and distance, dominance issues, and many other feelings of tension and suffering. On top of that, the result of anger often invites feelings of negativity towards us. This is why we are told to never let the sun go down on our anger:

Let not the sun go down upon your wrath. (Ephesians 4:26)

Another reason why we should never let the sun go down on our anger is the effect it has on us. It can cause us restless sleep, bad dreams, fogginess, vengeful and bitter thoughts, or even affect our mental, emotional, and physical well-being.

Appendix II: Secondary Practices 155

The first step in overcoming anger is to recognize how it unbalances us. The next step is to consider the many guises anger manifests as. Below is a small list of the different ways anger can be expressed:

- Explosive or implosive
- Misdirected as when venting on someone or something that is not directly connected with the anger
- Repressing it until it eats us from inside out
- Bitterness
- Role playing hurtful or harmful thoughts
- Turn it upon ourselves.
- Becoming angrier because we are angry
- Irritable
- Mumbling
- Resentment
- Vengeance
- Passive aggressiveness like the silent treatment
- Being vindictive or talking negatively about others
- Putting people down
- Acting in a way that causes others harm
- Stealing or hiding things
- Manipulating
- Provoking
- Withholding things
- Self-blame
- Self-harm
- Negative indifference
- Depression
- Excessiveness
- Threatening
- Yelling
- Blaming
- Physical violence
- Biting jokes
- Getting in peoples space
- Bullying
- Poking at people's weaknesses
- Speaking incomprehensibly

- Tunnel vision
- Not able to think logically
- Making general accusations
- Aggressive body language
- Continually coming back to the same perspective irrespective of other viewpoints
- Etc.

Those are a few ways anger presents itself. Once we see the way anger manifests in our lives then we need to get at the root of it. Why are we angry?

- Hurt feelings
- Alone
- Scared
- Frustrated
- Not being listen to
- Not being respected
- Not understanding
- Not getting what we want
- Ignorance
- Impatience
- Over-burdened
- Unfairly treated
- Being taken advantage of
- Not being appreciated
- Lacking in something
- Not dexterous or skilled enough
- Jealous
- Awkward
- Embarrassed
- Vulnerable
- Etc.

When we look at the source of anger what we find is either feelings of vulnerability or lack of control. Now that we know our justifications, how it manifests in our lives, and what the source is: what are we to do with that information? Working with anger is not easy. It is not something that disappears once we have won over it a couple of times. It is a practice that comes up over and over and over and over and over again. James gives us advice when he tells us:

> *Let every man be swift to hear, slow to speak, slow to wrath.* (James 1:19)

One way to be swift in listening is to be quick in recognizing when we are vulnerable to anger. Below are some common situations that can make us vulnerable:

- Tired
- Hot
- In a hurry
- Hungry
- Overwhelmed
- Trying to concentrate
- Lots of commotion or confusion
- Have a deadline
- Uncertain how to do something
- In uncomfortable setting or situation
- Where possible danger is
- When depending upon others
- When trying to convey information to another
- When trying to understand something
- Being taken advantage of
- Being overlooked
- Etc.

Being slow to speak tells us that we should never act without consideration. Take a moment to see clearly into the situation. Most times when anger arises it is due to some form of ignorance: not being able to see the whole picture, not understanding where the other person is coming from, or not clearly understanding what is expected of us. Slow to anger of course is telling us to stay our anger. Find another way to relate with the situation. Come up with an alternate solution, keep the mind open and listen to what is really going on. All these things help us deal with anger. In proverbs we are told:

A soft answer turneth away wrath. (15:1)

Gentleness is the surest way to deal with anger – either when it is directed towards us or when we see it arising within ourselves. Gentleness opens enough room for anger to dissipate. It takes away the heat of the fire while allowing the light of the flame to remain.

Anger affects us not only during its rein, but long after it's gone. It is not something that uplifts the heart but rather burns it. While there are many reasonable justifications for anger and even useful techniques in helping us overcome certain weaknesses, in reality, anger is a dangerous ally that should be used only sparingly, if not at all.

Some things that happens while being angry

- Stomach in knots
- Body is restless
- Thoughts are tunneled
- Blood pressure is up
- Shortness of breath
- Trembling
- Heighten senses
- Stiffness of posture
- Contracted pupils
- Increased physical strength
- Lack of coordination
- Sweaty palms, armpits, etc.
- Release of adrenaline and other hormones
- Intense emotions
- Motion is jerky and unpredictable
- Externalization of blame
- Etc.

Some things that happen after an anger episode

- Thoughts are either frustrated, clouded, empty, or jittery
- Restless and on edge
- Judgmental
- Depression
- Self-blame
- Anxiety
- Tired and drained
- Agitated and frustrated
- Hatred
- Constipation or diarrhea
- Heart murmurs
- Sweating
- Confusion
- Listless
- Frazzled
- Irritable
- Difficulty sleeping
- Restless sleep
- Etc.

Things to contemplate

"For the wrath of man worketh not the righteousness of God." (James 1:20)
- Define anger.
- Why does the wrath of man not work the righteousness of GOD?
- What is the righteousness of GOD?
- Can anger be good? Explain.

"Let not the sun go down upon your wrath." (Ephesians 4:26)
- What is this verse saying to you?
- Why is it important to deal with anger rather than let it simmer?
- Name three times in your life when anger was allowed to simmer. What happened?

"Let every man be swift to hear, slow to speak, slow to wrath." (James 1:19)
- Name ten different triggers in your life that invite anger.

- How could being slow to speak or react be helpful in those situations?
- How can being swift to hear help with anger?

"A soft answer turneth away wrath" (Proverbs 15:1)
- How can softness and gentleness help turn away anger?
- Has there ever been a time in your life when someone spoke softly and kindly to you while you were enraged? If so, what were the results, feelings, and thoughts that arose because of it?
- Can being soft and gentle be the answer for all situations? Explain.
- Is this verse talking about using gentleness with yourself or with someone that is wrathful towards you? Explain.

Practices to help work with anger

- Consider the things you have done before which are similar to those things you are angry with now.
- Figure out why you are angry. Not the external action or situation that triggered the anger, but the actual source. For example: hurt, disappointed, vulnerable, etc.
- Make a list of everyone you are angry with and explain why.
- Make a list of everyone who might be angry with you and explain why.
- Understand that there is no guarantee anger will create positive results. Simply consider how you feel and react when someone is angry with you to understand this point.
- Contemplate how you felt and what resulted from past times of anger.
- Every time anger arises make an effort to stop it. It might take many times, and sometimes while you are angry you might be aware of your anger as if watching it from a third person perspective, but still unable to prevent the anger from boiling over. Each time you work with this you will find yourself a little less out of control.
- Do positive affirmations to help.
- Become conscious that there is a problem. This awareness will slowly create a strong desire to overcome anger. Once the desire has arisen, work with these other techniques to help you lessen anger's control.

- Come up with a plan. If a certain situation continues to give rise to anger, then come up with an alternate plan to implement when this situation arises in the future.
- Make a list of all the things that make you angry in life.
- Continual condition yourself with whatever practice you find helpful.
- Create an actual desire to change and know that you have the power to do so.
- Replace anger with compassion.
- Stop the blame game and start to look at what is going on inside yourself.
- Let go of the other person or situation and look directly at the anger. By letting go of the storyline and relating to the actual emotion you can really begin to transform the energy into something else.
- Recognize the triggers and train yourself to be stronger whenever they arise.
- Work with meditation and other relaxation techniques.
- Avoid setting yourself up.
- Always try something new.
- Look from another perspective.
- Try laughing at yourself.
- Distract yourself from the situation until the initial energy has worn out.

Love

> *I in them, and thou in me, that they may be made perfect in one; and that the world may know that thou hast sent me, and hast loved them, as thou hast loved me. (John 17:23)*

Love calms the wild beast, turns evil from its course, opens the hardest heart, awakens the soul from darkness, and brings to life those who slumber. While this text avoids mystical practices, to talk about love is to summon the mystical and the miraculous. This chapter will stay to common experience and leave the mystical practices to the third and final book of the Path of Christ series.

When researching you will find many beliefs about love: there are scientists who claim love does not exist, while some philosophers will say that life would not be without it. We say love is this or that, a chemical or even an illusion, but when love has been felt all other experiences dim in comparison. Love is something that takes us beyond ourselves, and yet, brings us to the very essence of ourselves. It changes the world as we know it. It invites openness, kindness, joy, abundance, well-being, and unlimited happiness, while ridding us of hatred, anger, malice, impatience, pride, arrogance, selfishness, and separation.

Sometimes love is confused or intertwined with other feelings and emotions. Many look to love as a way to express lust, greed, selfishness, attachment, and other such emotions that bind, crave, desire, cling, and attach to. While each share a small part in love, love is something that stretches beyond thought and word. In its perfection love is GOD:

> *God is love; and he that dwelleth in love dwelleth in God, and God in him. (1 John 4:16)*

That's when love is no longer colored by the cloudiness of selfishness, fear, loneliness, desire, ignorance, or any other limited emotion. When love is in our hearts there is no fear or need for anything other than love itself.

> *There is no fear in love; but perfect love casteth out fear: because fear hath torment. He that feareth is not made perfect in love. (1 John 4:18)*

How can we invite love if we have no idea what it is? To start with, we should wish good-will to everyone. To ourselves and those we love, to friends, strangers, and even our enemies.

> *But I say unto you, love your enemies, bless them that curse you, do good to them that hate you, and pray for them which despitefully use you, and persecute you. (Matthew 5:44)*

Just like the compassion practice earlier in the text, the practice of sending love opens us to all things. When we can send love with all our heart and mind, then we can do what Jesus tells us in Matthew:

> **Thou shalt love the Lord thy God with all thy heart, and with all thy soul, and with all thy mind.** *(22:37)*

Until we can love our neighbor (1 John 4:20), there is no way we can love GOD fully and completely. When we can, we will be able to lay our life down for others; for there is no greater sign of Love than giving our life to another (John 15:13).

Things to contemplate

"I in them, and thou in me, that they may be made perfect in one; and that the world may know that thou hast sent me, and hast loved them, as thou hast loved me." (John 17:23)

- Define love.
- Research love and write down ten definitions of love.
- What does this verse say about love?
- What does 'I in them and thou in me' mean?

"God is love; and he that dwelleth in love dwelleth in God, and God in him." (1 John 4:16)

- Why is GOD love?
- What does this verse and the above verse have in common?
- How does love unite you with that which you love?

"There is no fear in love; but perfect love casteth out fear: because fear hath torment. He that feareth is not made perfect in love." (1 John 4:18)

- Make a list of some different qualities of love.
- What is unconditional love?
- How can perfect love cast out fear?
- Is jealousy part of love?
- Does love depend on anything? Explain answer.

"But I say unto you, love your enemies, bless them that curse you, do good to them that hate you, and pray for them which despitefully use you, and persecute you." (Matthew 5:44)

- How can you love those who hate you?
- Why would you ever want to love others?
- What good does loving your enemies do?

"Thou shalt love the Lord thy God with all thy heart, and with all thy soul, and with all thy mind." (Matthew 22:37)

- What does all your heart mean?
- What does all your soul mean?
- What does all your mind mean?

Practices to help invite love

- Every time you hear a siren, answer the phone, or in any way find yourself in communication with another person, mentally verbalize, 'May mercy be upon you, and may peace and love multiply in your life.' Loosely quoted from (Jude 1:2).
- Do the love sending meditation as follows:
    1. Send love to yourself. Begin by doing the inner smile meditation which is basically considering each part of your body and sending a smile to it. Consider your organs and body parts. Really send love to yourself – especially those areas of your life that you do not like. Next visualize yourself in a joyful place and space and then send yourself love by saying, "May I be free of suffering, pain, and sadness and may joy, abundance, and love grow within my life."
    2. Send love to those dear to you: partners, children, friends, etc. Visualize them in a happy and joyful place as your send to them the following thoughts, "May you be free of suffering, pain, and sadness while joy, abundance, and love grow in your life."
    3. Do step two for strangers and enemies. Make sure to visualize them in a joyful and happy place as you send them the words and energy.
    4. Finish the love sending meditation by extending it out to the ten directions. Send love to the four primary direction: east, west, north, and south. Send love to the secondary directions: northeast, northwest, southeast, and

southwest. Send love to the tertiary directions: above and below.
5. Once every direction and everyone has been sent love, take all that love and send it to GOD as you say, "I love you with all my heart, body, mind, and soul. Everything I am and have I give to you. Amen"

Forgiving

> *Be ye kind one to another, tenderhearted, forgiving one another, even as God for Christ's sake hath forgiven you. (Ephesians 4:32)*

While forgiveness is not the sole property of Christianity, we could say that no other religion or philosophy has developed it more than Jesus. Forgiveness is not a weakness, nor is it a means to control or manipulate us. If we continually find ourselves becoming a victim because we forgive, than something is wrong. Forgiveness liberate us from suffering – it does not surround us with it. The teaching to forgive seven times seven in Matthew 18:22 has been pushed into our minds so often that a church, teacher, organization, or government can do the most horrendous acts without consequence – as if we are suppose to forgive and allow these acts to continue. We are told in Matthew 18:15-17 to confront those that sin and if that does not work then we are to bring together a few others or even the congregation in the hopes of turning them away from their transgressions. If that does not work, then we are told to lay aside the relationship.

While there seems to be a contradiction between these two verses above, in essence they are congruent. To forgive from the heart does not mean we have to stay in an unhealthy relationship and continue to be abused, taken advantage of, or harmed. To forgive from the heart is what we seek. Sometimes distance and separation is the very thing we need in order to find that.

Forgiveness is at the root of Christianity. In essence it is one of the unique contributions Christianity has given to the world. In no other religion do we find this concept of freeing ourselves from our past merely by the act of forgiving those who have acted against us. The catch to this is repentance. While it would be easy to say, "I forgive a murderer for killing in order to justify killing myself." This is wrongful thinking. If forgiveness comes from the depth of the heart there will follow a repentance of the soul which guides us away from such actions. True forgiveness is a Divine act. When we forgive we are reaching deep within ourselves and disentangling the strings, emotions, thoughts, memories, and feelings connected with an experience. We let go of ourselves and allow the Divine to move through us.

In life and especially with the Path, there are many levels and reasons behind the actions we do. This applies to forgiveness as well. Just as with faith, there are many degrees of forgiveness:

- *Superficial* (When someone forgives merely to end strife or because they are told to do so)
- *Conditioned* (When someone forgives because they were conditioned to do so)
- *Self-interest* (When someone forgives to gain something: power, control, harmony, sex, etc.)
- *Regretful* (Forgiving because the result of an action is not what was intended)
- *Guilt* (Forgiving because guilt or shame has arisen from our actions)
- *Sorry* (A feeling of forgiveness that is said in the spur of the moment after an accident: bumping into someone, taking something that was someone else's unaware, and so on – this is light and sincere)
- *Apologetic* (A genuine feeling of forgiveness that arises after thinking deeply about the consequences of our actions)
- *Concerned* (A genuine feeling of forgiveness that is rooted in a deep feeling of concern and compassion)
- *Spiritual* (Perfect forgiveness that is rooted in the very nature of the Divine which forgives completely and unconditionally)

While looking at forgiveness in this way is superficial, it does give us a gauge to work with when we begin to practice forgiving others. The first step in forgiving is to know ourselves. Who are we, what do we think, feel, perceive, etc? We do this to help us see that we have no right to throw the first stone, and so, it opens the way for us to truly forgive ourselves and others.

Below are twelve groups of questions that will help you learn about yourself. The reason these questions are so important in forgiveness is that it helps us see within ourselves the things we do and believe. The more aware we are of our own weaknesses, harmful ways, beliefs and actions, the more forgiving we become. We are told to forgive so we will be forgiven in Matthew 6:15, this can only come when we know what it means to be forgiven. Self-knowledge is the easiest way to open our hearts to this understand. If we can forgive ourselves, then truly we can forgive others.

Questions on initiation and perception:
- How do you start things? Do you need to be pushed, pulled, motivated, etc…
- How do you perceive society?
- How does society perceive you?
- How does life treat you?

Questions on security and self identity:
- Who are you?
- What do you like to spend money on?
- How do you feel about money?
- What do you think about people who have everything handed to them on a silver spoon? What about those who have nothing?
- Where do you find safety, security, stability?
- What do you value?
- What do you identify with?
- What materials define you?
- What do you hold onto as your core identity?
- How is your self-esteem?

Questions on beliefs and the thinking process:
- What are your core beliefs?
- What things do you have a strong opinion about?
- What do you like to learn and explore?
- What do you think about often?
- What thought process do you use? Example: linear, symbolic, artistic, mathematical, cluster, etc...
- How would you define your mind? Example: cloudy, fuzzy, clear, slow, fast, etc...
- What does knowledge mean to you?
- What happens to your thoughts when:
    1. Being confronted
    2. Yelled at
    3. Worrying over something
    4. Contemplating
    5. Fantasying
    6. Having to explain something
    7. When someone is not listening to you
    8. When you feel disrespected
    9. Desiring
- How do you learn? Example: Visual, tactile, hearing, mental, etc...
- What major things come to mind when you think about your early childhood?

Questions on home, family, and how you get what you want:
- Where do you go or what do you do when things get overwhelming?
- What was your home life like?
- What does Home mean to you?
- What kind of subtle ways do you use to get what you want?
- How do you relate to your mother?
- What does a mom represent to you?
- How do you create your home?
- How do you resolve issues in your life?
- Write out your life history?
- Consider these things of your past
    1. Things missed
    2. Things that were not liked
    3. What you wished were different
    4. Some fears
    5. Reoccurring dreams

6. What you wanted to be when you grew up
7. Some compromises you had to make
8. Pets
9. Friends

Questions on hobbies, entertainment, adventures, children:
- What does romance mean?
- What kinds of people excite you?
- How do you view children?
- What does parenting mean to you?
- Where do you go over the top?
- What does freedom mean to you?
- How would you use more leisure time?
- What hobbies do you have?
- How do you compete?
- Where do you express your creativity?
- Where do you seek to be recognized?

Questions on work, responsibility, and priorities:
- What are your priorities?
- What kinds of things do you carry on your shoulders without wanting help from others?
- What does it mean to be healthy?
- What kinds of food do you like and why?
- What are your routines?
- What kind of work do you like and dislike and why?
- How do you approach work?
- Is work and home life separate or do you keep in contact with those you work with in your home life?
- How do you handle authority?
- How do you handle being bossed around and what kinds of feelings arise when it happens?
- How do you relate to pets and what pets do you like?
- Where do you try to be perfect?
- Where do you slack off?
- How do you take care of yourself?
- How do you deal with sickness?
- How do you feel about needy people?
- How do you handle responsibility?

Questions about relationships:
- How do new relationships begin in your life?
- What qualities do you look for in a partner?
- What does marriage mean to you?
- How do you feel and deal with being dependent upon others?
- How do you feel and deal with those that depend on you?
- What kind of people do you see as your enemy?
- What do you expect in a relationship?
- What do you accept in a relationship?
- What kinds of things do you project on others?
- What qualities or character traits do you have a hard time dealing with? In yourself and in others?
- What personification do you project in a group setting?
- What kinds of things do you sacrifice for those you care about?
- How might your friends perceive you?

Questions on death, instincts, emotions, and sex:
- What do you think most other people value?
- What beliefs do you have about death?
- What kind of feelings and thoughts arise when contemplating death?
- How do you feel about the trials in your life? Why did they happen?
- What role do instincts play in your life?
- What role does greed, jealousy, passion, lust, and power play in your life?
- What major kinds of conscious shifts have happened in your life?
- What does having control mean to you?
- How do you feel about sex?
- How is sex used in the advertisement business? Explain.
- What kinds of major separations have you had in your life?

Questions on learning and religion:
- What are some major religious and philosophical beliefs you hold onto?
- What do you think about the news?
- How do you go about learning things?
- How do you find meaning in your life?
- What things do you like to learn about? Why?

- Where would you like to travel and why?
- What does spirituality mean to you?
- What would your life be like without spirituality?

Questions about the father and how you fit into the bigger picture:
- What was/is your relationship like with your father?
- What does the dad archetype represent to you?
- How do you behave in public versus private?
- How do you want the world to see you?
- What do you wish to be recognized and admired for?
- How do you go about making things better in the world?
- What do you believe your destiny is?
- What are some of your ambitions?
- What drives your life?

Questions on socialization:
- What kinds of friends do you look for?
- What kinds of groups, clubs, organizations, etc. do you gravitate towards?
- What kind of qualities do you expect in your friends?
- What archetypal role do you fill in your friendships?
- How do you deal with having to work in a group setting?
- What is a perfect society to you mean?
- What kinds of things do you visualize in your life?
- What things stimulate your creativity?

Questions on transcendence and the shadow things of life:
- What is the highest union possible in life?
- What kinds of things do you lose yourself to?
- What does wholeness mean?
- How do you feel about suicide?
- How has drugs and alcohol impacted your life?
- How do you feel about drugs and alcohol?
- What things confuse you?
- How do you conform?
- Where do you set your boundaries?
- How do you escape and what pushes you to do it?
- What kinds of dilemmas arise within your life?
- How do you view dreams? What do you dream?

Now that we know a little bit about ourselves and what really goes on inside – who are we to throw the first stone? We are told that unless we forgive those who trespass against us, GOD will not forgive us. How much do we need that forgiveness?

Things to contemplate

"Be ye kind one to another, tenderhearted, forgiving one another, even as God for Christ's sake hath forgiven you." (Ephesians 4:32)
- What does forgiveness mean?
- How does forgiveness work?
- Make a list of things you have been forgiven for in the past.
- Make a list of all the people you have forgiven in the past.

"Moreover if thy brother shall trespass against thee, go and tell him his fault between thee and him alone: if he shall hear thee, thou hast gained thy brother. But if he will not hear thee, then take with thee one or two more, that in the mouth of two or three witnesses every word may be established. And if he shall neglect to hear them, tell it unto the church: but if he neglect to hear the church, let him be unto thee as a heathen man and a publican." (Matthew 18:15-17)
- How do you forgive?
- Is forgiveness healthy or harmful? Explain.
- How does it feel when being forgiven?
- How does it feel to forgive?

"Jesus saith unto him, I say not unto thee, until seven times: but, until seventy times seven." (Matthew 18:22)
- What is this verse saying?
- How does this verse relate to family?
- Is this verse telling you to stay in a relationship that constantly abuses you over and over again? Explain.

Practices to help invite forgiveness

- Every time you find yourself confronted with certain emotions towards others take the opportunity to look at yourself and then forgive.

- Answer the twelve groups of questions and consider what areas in your life you have a hard time forgiving others. Does it have any relation to your own issues and experiences?
- Every time a negative thought or feeling arises about someone, consciously send them love and your blessing. Stop the thinking before it builds strength. Take that initial energy and forgive. Open your heart to love and joy rather than bitterness and pain. And again, just because you forgive does not mean you condone. It just means you let go of the pain and suffering.
- Write down all your pain, anger, bitterness, and hatred on a piece of paper. Make sure to spell out everything you are feeling. Then burn the paper while praying/meditating to help you overcome these things. Do this until you feel the pain lessening. This is a technique meant to be used only at the very beginning. Sometimes pain needs to be recognized and acknowledged, least it gets buried and end up coming back later to haunt you. Once the initial anger has distanced itself, then you can begin to work with sending love.
- Consider similar things you have done and the reasons behind them. Would you not also want to be forgiven? Do you believe you deserve it? Explain.
- Make forgiveness a practice. Go through your whole life and send forgiveness to everyone that has caused you harm. By doing this you are opening yourself up to forgiveness. It is the law of cause and effect. What you sow is what you reap. Start with things that are easily forgivable. That way you will be building upon a foundation of forgiving instead of shooting for the moon with a BB gun.

Prayer

> ***Pray without ceasing.*** *(1 Thessalonians 5:17)*

The first thing we need to do is define prayer. We can go crazy trying to say what prayer is and what it is not. In essence prayer is simply communing with GOD. We can do this constantly by bringing to mind GOD in all things that we do. As 1 Thessalonians 5:17 teaches us, we should always have our mind directed towards GOD and look for GOD'S guidance in everything we do. Every moment and in every place we should lift our hearts to GOD (1 Timothy 2:8). The Eastern Orthodox

Tradition prays without ceasing by using the Jesus Prayer as a type of mantra until it forever resides within the heart and mind. This and similar practices will be talked about in the second book of the Path of Christ series. For now the idea of prayer without ceasing is simply to have GOD within our hearts and minds as often as possible.

So how do we pray? It can be said that prayer utilizes many techniques of meditation. We are to silence our senses, clear the mind, open the heart, let go of any thoughts that arise, avoid visualizations of any kind, and simply become aware of GOD's presence within us. Once we have cleared our minds of all distractions and begun to commune with GOD, it is necessary to open ourselves up and listen. Will we hear a voice, see images, etc? Yes. Are they connected to GOD? Who knows? We are told by saints and monks to test the spirit and see if they are good or bad. We do this by questioning. Does it lead us to selfish ends, cause harm, drive us towards riches or power, or anything else that goes against what Jesus taught? GOD works in mysterious ways, so who are we to say how or when GOD works in our lives. If we invoke the Divine in our prayers and have cleared our minds of all thoughts, then we have minimized the chances of being mislead.

Some different reasons for prayer
- Praise
- Requests and petitions
- Guidance
- Confession and consolation
- Overcoming pain or suffering
- Protection
- Strength and courage
- Expression of what is going on
- Self-knowledge
- Overcoming temptations
- Transformation
- Healing
- Miracles
- Wisdom and understanding

- Communion
- Union
- Bliss
- Etc…

The first step in prayer is to define our intention. Why are we praying? Once we understand the why then we can begin the actual process of praying. We are told in Matthew 6:6 to enter our closet, close our doors, and pray to GOD which is in secret. What is this saying – to hide under our clothes? Maybe, but most likely it is telling us to enter our heart which is our closet, shut our doors which are the five senses, and pray to GOD who is secreted within us.

> *When thou prayest, enter into thy closet, and when thou hast shut thy door, pray to thy Father which is in secret; and thy Father which seeth in secret shall reward thee openly.* (Matthew 6:6)

This is a lot easier said than done. For one, the moment we find ourselves closing our eyes to pray, a million images, thoughts, and feelings arise. In all that turmoil what hope is there for us to connect with the Divine. This is one reason why meditation is vitally important. It helps us silence our internal dialog so that we can pray. If you have done the practices in this text and begun working with meditation as instructed in chapter six, then you're already on your way to calming the mind.

> *When ye stand praying, forgive, if ye have ought against any.* (Mark 11:25)

Forgiveness is very important to prayer. If we have something against our neighbor there will be a residue of anger and frustration that will constantly distract and deter us from prayer. This energy is something that has to be let go of before we can enter into our hearts.

> *Watch and pray, that ye enter not into temptation: the spirit indeed is willing, but the flesh is weak.*
> (Matthew 26:41)

Always keep a vigilant awareness of what is going on in the mind. The more comfortable we are with our prayers the more vulnerable we become. The mind has infinite ways of distracting us. The closer we get to GOD the more the ego distracts us – for the touch of GOD is the ego's demise. Sometimes temptation might even disappeared for a time, which leads us to believe that we have overcome our fleshly desires only to later reappear as pride or self-gratifying emotions and thoughts.

> *But when ye pray, use not vain repetitions, as the heathen do: for they think that they shall be heard for their much speaking.* (Matthew 6:7)

Vain repetitions are another error many make in their prayers: "Please GOD! Please GOD! PLEASE GOD!" We should avoid pestering GOD for things like little children who seek to get what they want by annoying their parents. While there is no limit to GOD's patience, we often find ourselves learning patience when we pray in this way. If a desire for something is what we seek then simply using the Lord's Prayer is sufficient, because GOD knows what it is we need and want (Matthew 6:9-13).

> *And straightway the father of the child cried out, and said with tears, Lord, I believe; help thou mine unbelief.* (Mark 9:24)

While it is not talked about much in the scriptures, true prayer comes with tears. Humility is the key – not like the Pharisee who stood in the temple praying from his righteous pedestal, but as the publican who smote his breast and cried out in Luke 18:10-14.

Once we have an understanding of why we are praying, entered our heart and closed off our senses, forgiven those we have something against, set our minds to overcome all distractions, let go of any selfish repetition, and humbled ourselves, we are ready to pray. While there are formulaic techniques for posture, prostrations, and so forth, for the sake of this text we will simply direct the reader to do what comes natural to them. If we are too rigid in the beginning with our prayers we run the risk of losing the spirit of it, and if we become too lose, we run the risk of getting distracted. In the second text of the Path of Christ series we will go over a few different prayer formulas: for now – just pray as you see fit.

Things to contemplate

"Pray without ceasing." (1 Thessalonians 5:17)
- What is prayer?
- What does pray without ceasing mean?
- Why do you pray?

"When thou prayest, enter into thy closet, and when thou hast shut thy door, pray to thy Father which is in secret; and thy Father which seeth in secret shall reward thee openly." (Matthew 6:6)
- How does this verse teach you to pray?
- How does GOD reward openly?
- How does this verse differ from those who pray on the corners of the street?
- Is prayer necessary?

"When ye stand praying, forgive, if ye have ought against any." (Mark 11:25)
- Why is forgiving necessary for prayer?
- How can animosity interfere with your prayers?
- How can prayer help you forgive others?

"But when ye pray, use not vain repetitions, as the heathen do: for they think that they shall be heard for their much speaking." (Matthew 6:7)
- What do you think this verse is saying?
- Why is "vain repetitions" specified instead of just *repetitions*? What is the difference?

- Can you ask for the same thing in different ways and get away with avoiding vain repetition? Explain.

"And straightway the father of the child cried out, and said with tears, Lord, I believe; help thou mine unbelief." (Mark 9:24)
- When you pray do you cry?
- Do you cry at all?
- How do you feel about crying? Explain.
- Why are tears a sign of humility?
- Why would crying be necessary for deep prayer?
- What is crying good for?
- What are some reasons for crying? Tears of joy, desolation, etc?
- Is it okay to cry? Explain.

Praying

- Set aside a certain time in your day to pray.
- Do not forget to be spontaneous and pray throughout the day.
- Steps of Prayer:
    1. *Entrance:* Setting the intention (Hebrews 4:12)
    2. *Withdrawing:* Close your doors and enter into your abode (Matthew 6:6)
    3. *Silencing:* Silencing all the mind stuff (Mark 4:39)
    4. *Reaching:* Calling out through prayer, seeking to find, knocking so it shall be opened (Matthew 7:7)
    5. *Opening:* Letting go of yourself so you can open to GOD (Matthew 10:39)
    6. *Yearning:* Seeking with all the heart and mind (Matthew 22:37)
    7. *Receiving:* Being touched by the Spirit (John 20:22)
    8. *Cleaving:* Connecting yourself and holding with all your heart and mind to GOD (Acts 11:23 & Matthew 19:5)
    9. *Union:* No longer feeling separated from GOD (1 Corinthians 6:17)

Appendix III
Essential Teachings of Jesus

Unlike the last two appendixes, this one has very little to say. If you take your time and really study and contemplate on these teachings you will find in many ways this appendix summarizing the whole path of Christ. If these quotes can be memorized then the essence of Christianity will be infused within you.

Letting go
- If any man will come after me, let him deny himself, and take up his cross and follow me
- Verily I say unto you, except ye be converted, and become as little children, ye shall not enter unto the kingdom of heaven
- Let anyone who is flawless, throw the first stone
- Take heed, and beware of covetousness: for a man's life consisteth not in the abundance of the things which he possesses
- The life is more than meat, and the body is more than raiment
- Thy Will be done, not mine

Gratitude
- The very hairs of your head are all numbered
- I thank you, O Father, Lord of heaven and earth, because thou hast hid these things from the wise and prudent and hast revealed them unto babes.
- In everything give thank

Focus
- Lay up for yourselves treasures in heaven. For where your treasure is, there will your heart be also.
- The light of the body is the eye: if therefore thine eye be single, thy whole body shall be full of light.

External Practices
- Faith, if it hath not works, is dead, being alone
- On the good ground are they, which in an honest and good heart, having heard the word, keep it, and bring forth fruit with patience
- What measure you mete it shall be measured unto you again

- Let him that stole steal no more
- Every idle word that men shall speak, they shall give account thereof in the Day of Judgment
- Give to him that asketh thee
- Love your enemies, bless them that curse you, do good to them that hate you, and pray for them which despitefully use you, and persecute you
- Do not premeditate but allow the spirit to speak through you
- When thy do they alms, let not thy left hand know what thy right hand doeth. When ye fast, be not, as the hypocrites, of a sad countenance; for they disfigure their faces that they may appear unto men to fast. Anoint thine head, and wash thy face; that thou appear not unto men to fast, but unto the Father, which seeth in secret, shall reward thee openly. When thou prayest, enter into thy closet and when thou hast shut thy door, pray to thy Father which is in secret; and thy Father which seeth in secret shall reward thee openly
- That ye resist not evil: but whosoever shall smite thee on thy right cheek, turn to him the other also. And if any man will sue thee at the law, and take away thy coat, let him have thy cloak also

Inner Practices

- Cleanse first that which is within the cup and platter, that the outside of them may be clean also
- All they that take the sword shall perish by the sword
- That whosoever looketh on a woman to lust by them hath committed adultery with her already in his heart
- Not that which goeth into the mouth defileth a man; but that which cometh out of the mouth, this defileth a man
- For if you love them which love you, what reward have ye? Do not even the publicans the same? And if ye salute your brethren only, what do you have more than others? Do not even the publicans so? Be ye therefore perfect, even as your Father which is in heaven is perfect
- Watch and pray, that ye enter not into temptation: the spirit indeed is willing, but the flesh is weak
- Godliness with contentment is great gain. For we brought nothing into this world, and it is certain that we will carry nothing out. And having food and raiment, let us be therewith content. But they that will be rich fall into temptation and a snare, and into many foolish and hurtful lusts, which drown men in destruction and perdition. For the love of money is the root of all evil: which while some

coveted after, they have erred from the faith, and pierced themselves through with many sorrows

Humility
- He that is greatest among you shall be your servant
- For everyone that exalteth himself shall be abased, and he that humbleth himself shall be exalted

Wisdom
- Know ye not that your body is the temple of the Holy Ghost
- Blessed are the poor in spirit: for theirs is the kingdom of heaven
- Blessed are they that mourn: for they shall be comforted
- Blessed are the meek: for they shall inherit the earth.
- Blessed are they which do hunger and thirst after righteousness: for they shall be filled
- Blessed are the merciful: for they shall obtain mercy.
- Blessed are the pure in heart: for they shall see GOD
- Blessed are the peacemakers: for they shall be called the children of GOD
- Behold, the Kingdom of God is within you.

Appendix III: Forty Essential Teachings of Jesus

Ways to connect with Jesus by seeing him as:

1. Savior
2. Farmer
3. Carpenter
4. Bridegroom
5. Fisher
6. Healer
7. Baker
8. King
9. Servant
10. Landowner
11. Friend
12. Liberator
13. Son of GOD
14. Priest
15. Teacher
16. Anointed One
17. Herder
18. Brother
19. Guide
20. Supporter
21. GURU
22. Gateway – Doorway – Pathway
23. Aspect of GOD, etc…

Four Poisons:	Antidotes:
Anger	Letting Go
Hatred	Love
Fear	Faith
Desire	Contentment

Bibliography

Gźon-nu-rgyal-mchog, Dkon-mchog-rgyal-mtshan, and Jinpa Thupten. *Mind Training: The Great Collection*. Boston, MA: Wisdom Publications, in Association with the Institute of Tibetan Classics, 2006. Print.

King James Bible. Nashville, TN: Holman Bible, 1973. Print.

A Different Road:
From Bum to Mystic

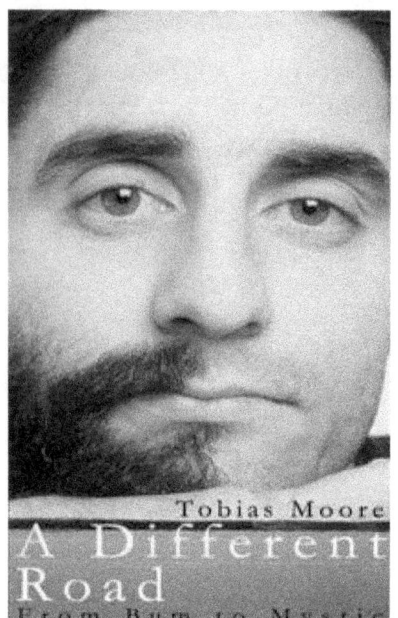

Learn about what made me into who I am. Read about the experiences, people, and thoughts that gave form to my understandings of Life and the Spirit. This is my story, at least, part of my story – the crazy part. This book takes some of my more exciting adventures I experienced during my six plus years traveling the United States: Rainbow Gatherings, Grateful Dead and Phish Shows, Underground Punk Movement, and the Occult World were just a few of those adventures.

Available from Amazon.com and other retailers!

ABOUT THE AUTHOR

I live in the mountains, I have five children, and I am ever grateful for the blessings I have. I love gardening, talking with spirits, doing rituals, playing with my kids, reading, learning, and otherwise enjoying the little bit of time I have here on earth. My life's wish, besides living in a sacred manner and having a family, is to buy a piece of land, grow my own food, live off the grid, and write about my spiritual pursuits in the hopes of sharing my experiences and practices with others. Visit www.sohmpublishing.com for information on upcoming titles and blog entries expounding on the *Path of Christ* and other topics.

www.ingramcontent.com/pod-product-compliance
Lightning Source LLC
Chambersburg PA
CBHW051756040426
42446CB00007B/394